LOW-COST
GARDENING

GARDEN MATTERS

LOW-COST GARDENING

IAN G. WALLS

WARD LOCK

First published in Great Britain in 1992
by Ward Lock Limited, Villiers House,
41/47 Strand, London WC2N 5JE, England

A Cassell Imprint

© Ward Lock

Text filmset in ITC Garamond
by Columns Design and Production Services Ltd, Reading
Printed and bound in Great Britain by
HarperCollins Manufacturing, Glasgow

British Library Cataloguing in Publication Data
Walls, Ian G. (Ian Gascoigne), *1922–*
Low-cost gardening – (Garden matters)
I. Title   II. Series
635

ISBN 0–7063–7025–2

CONTENTS

PREFACE

Gardening, while always a vital part of life in Britain, has escalated considerably as a hobby in recent years. There is no way to develop or look after a garden and enjoy it actively and positively without spending money. Sales of gardening commodities have, in consequence, shown a dramatic rise. It must be said that gardening, like many other things, has become more expensive in recent years.

Low-Cost Gardening looks at things from a practical, down-to-earth angle. It points the way to making savings, and at the same time avoid needless waste of money by buying your needs and gardening more intelligently.

IGW

AUTHOR'S NOTE

Prices given in this book are for general guidance only, and relate to spring 1991. Prices vary greatly around the country, especially for plant materials. Inflation must be taken into account with its inevitable effect on prices. The author is grateful to several firms for help with prices and comments. He would especially thank Duncans Garden Centre, Milngavie, Glasgow.

CHAPTER 1

SETTING THE SCENE

Britain is often called a nation of gardeners, simply because it has a high proportion of gardens linked to homes. The standard of upkeep and enthusiasm for gardens and gardening varies enormously, but it is clear there has been a massive surge in gardening interest over the last few years. The main reasons are: more leisure time; more home ownership and pride of possession; escalating retail spending in DIY spheres generally.

The strong 'green' campaign is also a factor for gardeners wanting to do their bit for the environment, and produce healthier food crops – in many cases, it must be said, at more cost and work than 'traditional' gardening!

This increased enthusiasm for gardening means that sales of gardening commodities have risen considerably, and it looks as if things will continue this way. It is remarkable how people turn to their gardens and allotments in times of stress. Many also see them as a source of food and help with the household budget.

GETTING THE BEST OUT OF YOUR GARDEN

Sensible buying, sensible planning, and planned activity are three key factors. Let's see the best way of achieving these objectives.

BUYING YOUR NEEDS

You can't run a garden on air. You need to buy plants and possibly tubs or furniture to put into it, tools to cultivate and operate it, fertilizers or organic manures to feed the plants. At the same time, problems of pests and diseases will arise. All this means you are going to have to spend money. It is a question of being highly discriminating in *how* you spend your money and where you spend it. Gardening commodities are sold mainly in garden centres and DIY centres, supermarkets, hardware shops and smaller nurseries.

In addition to general displays of goods and plants, there is often the 'hard sell', seasonally promoted with loss-leader items to induce customers over the door-step. There will also be special events or displays at bulb time, shrub planting time etc.

The horticultural industry in general tends to be highly reputable but be vigilant as there are some rogues out there.

GETTING ADVICE ABOUT BUYING AND GARDENING

It can be more difficult to get good, objective advice on gardening matters than one imagines. The emphasis with many supply centres is on *selling*. Nevertheless, some centres have an advice desk, and it is worth seeking these out. You can also get help from gardening magazines and specialist societies.

CHECKING ON PRICES

The more lavish a garden or DIY supply centre, the better stocked it will generally be but some centres tend to concentrate on more profitable lines and it can be difficult to get quite basic necessities. Prices are sometimes higher in the larger centres, but some of the supermarket groups set out to be highly competitive. It pays to take time and shop around.

BUYING TREES AND SHRUBS

Many garden centres buy in plant material from larger producers, often under contract. You may find that smaller nurseries sell direct to the public, and their prices can be keener. You may not get the range of varieties or the very best quality, but you can save a lot of money.

End of season clear-outs of plant material are an excellent way of getting bargains, provided you are sure of quality and condition. For example, roses and shrubs in containers can deteriorate after a certain time and must be sold off, otherwise they get root-bound. A root-bound plant tends to establish badly. Ask the sales assistant to let you inspect the roots, which should not be in a tight and congested spiral mass, or starting to turn brown and decayed looking. Leaves should be healthy and not yellow or wilting.

BUYING OTHER PLANTS

The quality and price of plants and vegetables vary enormously. Unit plant production, with each plant in a separate little section or container, is gradually becoming standard, but crowded, root-entwined communal containers nevertheless make very convenient selling units!

'In flower' plants for instant bedding are now much in demand, but you will pay more for them. There are various stages of plants, the cheapest being seedlings for growing on, if you have room to accommodate them. Look out for end-of-season sales of seeds. Many flower seeds are sold off at half price or less and can be good buys, especially as most seeds nowadays come in air-tight packaging. Many garden centres and supermarkets look after their plants very badly indeed. The cost for bedding plants can range from around 8p a plant to 70p or even more, and it will pay you to shop around (Chapter 7). Gardening groups are increasingly club-bing together for collective purchases, and savings of up to 25 per cent or more are possible.

Pot plants vary, too, in size and quality, and remember that a great majority of pot plants are now imported from overseas. Whatever you buy, check out precisely what you are paying per plant and what size and condition the plants are in. This will vary according to the care they have had. Look for strong, healthy, unmarked leaves.

PESTS AND DISEASES

Look out for pests and diseases, as it is pointless spending money on bad material. Most supply centres spray regularly for pests and diseases, but some are difficult to control. Blackspot on roses, for example, seems to be around all over the place, and red spider mite seems to be resistant to insecticides. Check foliage very carefully and take a magnifying glass along with you: some pests, such as red spider, are very tiny. Refer if necessary to the free coloured pest and disease charts available. More is said about pests and diseases in the Appendix.

KEY BUYING POINTS FOR PLANT MATERIALS

Age, size, foliar development and root development (especially with shrubs and trees in containers), free-dom from pests and diseases, price per plant are all vital issues. Take time to shop around, compare quality and prices, and consider collective buying.

BUYING COMMODITIES

These are offered for sale at many DIY garden centres, supermarkets, hardware stores, and other outlets. Prices vary greatly, despite recommended retail prices.

The best buys are usually in equipment such as lawn mowers or mechanical equipment, where there is stock clearance. There are often sales of composts and organic manures at the end of the season, but remember they should be stored in a cool place. Look out if you are buying a really cheap greenhouse, it may prove flimsy and not able to stand up to storms. However, a plastic greenhouse may be all you require, and you could save yourself a lot of money, particularly if you are prepared to take the plastic inside during the winter months. This will be discussed in more detail in Chapter 3.

Discoloured stock is often sold off at half price, but remember that plastic items which have been lying around in the sunlight can often go brittle.

MAIL ORDER BUYING

Mail order in the UK amounts to 5 per cent of total sales of gardening commodities, and surveys of mail order firms show that many give only medium service, while others excel. Buy tentatively at first and see what the service and quality is like before spending too much.

COLLECTIVE BUYING

There is a lot of interest these days in buying in bulk. Someone, unfortunately, has to do the work of ordering, receiving goods and also distributing. However, it can be a very money-saving way of buying commodities, and has limited application for plant material too. Ideally, it needs someone good at bookwork to keep records, and fit enough to handle bags and materials. Transport helps with distribution, and administrative expenses can generally be covered by a small service charge.

DOES GOING 'GREEN' COST MORE?

There is much publicity these days about organic gardening. There is much emphasis on shunning chemicals, whether they be pesticides, weed-killers, fertilizers or other chemical items.

It is really quite a confusing picture. On the one hand, the large chemical companies are out for your business, and advertise lavishly. On the other, organic enthusiasts preach the evils of using chemicals. You *can* possibly produce more nutritious and healthier crops if you go organic – it is a matter open to debate – but it could cost you quite a bit more in time and effort.

It is logical to take a balanced view of things, use chemicals safely, sensibly and only when required. At the same time, grow your crops with as much organic matter as you can reasonably obtain, prepare with composting, or can afford to buy. The benefit of this is not only to feed your plants but to keep soils in good physical condition.

COST-SAVING SUMMARY

Be prepared to shop around: be discriminating. Keep your eyes open for bargains. Think about joining a gardening group, not only for help and advice but for group buying. Don't rush out and buy the first things you see. Take time to assess costs, and talk to other gardeners about where they get the best bargains. It may be better to pay more and get a good reliable article and at the same time a bit of advice on what you are buying.

CHAPTER 2

ASSESSING YOURSELF AND YOUR GARDEN

Gardens are not things one generally sets out to acquire; they invariably come along with the home you buy. However, once acquired, there are decisions to make over style of garden: to give it over entirely to decorative plants, or to allow space for fruit and vegetables, to incorporate as many labour-saving schemes as possible, to concentrate on raising your own plants.

SIZE OF GARDEN AND LEVELS

A key issue is size and this will reflect on the cost of maintaining it. Big gardens are generally going to cost more to develop and to keep going. There is the bonus that they can be productive of fruits and vegetables, and this can make a big difference to the household budget.

Terrain can be important. A sloping site could mean a lot of levelling and possibly retaining walls. This costs money. Sloping gardens can be more difficult to work. A compromise is a rockery, and this can be expensive if you go for a very attractive stone. On the other hand, local stone or a demolished sandstone building near you, can make for a cheap rockery. At all events, there is a fair bit of work involved. The same is true of terracing, or levelling generally, when you are going to need bricks or stone.

Sloping sites often have drainage problems especially in the lower areas, where water has seeped down from higher up. These problems have a nasty habit of developing over the years and cost money to put right.

On the credit side, the well-drained sloping garden can be very attractive, and indeed more productive if it slopes to the south. The interest of a flat garden may be improved by building up raised beds, rockeries or other features.

SOIL TYPES

Of all the various considerations, the type of soil can be a major factor towards gardening enthusiasm and success. A lot depends on the type of soil inherent in the area. It may be sticky clay, or light and sandy. Whatever soil is like initially, regular supplies of organic matter can create a better structure. More is discussed about soils and fertility in Chapter 4. If newly built-on land was well-managed farmland, you are lucky. Sometimes, however, building operations disturb the natural levels, leaving a lot of infertile subsoil on top. This takes a long time to overcome. Variances in depth of good soil over the whole garden can affect drainage and fertility. Builders have a responsibility to leave you with a good layer of topsoil and if they have not done this, or is there is a local authority involved, try to get things put right. Starting off a garden with inferior soil is not only costly but soul destroying.

On a new site, it is remarkable what builders leave behind. With a new home, representations should be made to the builders concerned, or alternatively the local authority or owners should be consulted. It must be said, however, that bricks, stones and other oddments can come in useful when developing a new garden!

It is remarkable how ignorant many gardeners are about the soil in their gardens. The best way is to dig a few inspection holes. Take up a few fistfuls of soil and squeeze them hard. If the soil sticks together in a ball, you have a clay soil; if it crumbles and won't hold together you have a lighter sandy soil. Even the absolute novice can find out a lot with this approach and this will tell you how to tackle your garden.

If you feel unsure about judging soil, get hold of an experienced gardening friend, possibly even someone with farming connections, to give you a bit of on-the-spot advice. It may even pay to send off your soil for analysis.

Remember that chemical analysis to check for levels of nutrients is one thing. Checking out the physical characteristics is another, and can be more expensive. More is said about testing soil in Chapter 4.

WEEDS

Keep an eye open for weeds. Nasty weeds such as horsetail are in recession in winter and you don't know they are there! Lots of weeds are short-term annuals, largely surface-growing. Getting rid of them is not too much of a problem, especially if you are not averse to contact-type weed-killers. If, on the other hand, you come across bits of roots indicative of creeping weeds such as couch grass, coltsfoot, convolvulus or, worst of all, horsetail you have a very expensive or laborious problem to get things right. Where adjoining land or gardens have the same range of creeping weeds, you are not going to solve things unless there is a collective policy of weed control. Houses with a really bad weed problem are best avoided!

For help in identifying weeds, consult a good illustrated guide of wild flowers or garden weeds, or seek the help of a botany teacher, university lecturer, professional gardener or nurseryman.

DRAINAGE

Theoretically speaking, drainage on a new plot should not be a problem as this should have been taken care of during the development phase by the builders or developers. Problems can develop, however, and they can be costly to put right.

A crowbar pushed well into the soil can let surface moisture drain away. If the problem seems more serious, dig inspection holes about 60 cm (2 ft) deep and watch what happens. Note how quickly rainwater drains away. One problem can be finding an effective outlet. Try to figure out exactly *why* you have a draining problem. The main reasons are:

1. Drainage of water from higher or adjoining land.
2. Low-lying ground with no effective outlet.
3. Consolidated top and/or sub-soils.
4. Heavy sticky clay soils not sufficiently porous to let water through quickly enough.
5. General lack of drainage systems linked to suitable outlets.

If you cannot find an effective outlet, try digging a very deep sump hole filled with bricks and rubble to within 30 cm (1 ft) of the surface, and run plastic or clay drain tiles into this. It does not always work but is better than nothing. While you can do a lot yourself, it is sometimes cheaper to get a contractor to do the job for you, *seeking a firm estimate beforehand*.

LOCALITY, ASPECT AND EXPOSURE

The general climate of an area, along with aspect and exposure, is often overlooked. Climate tends to be very much a regional affair. In general terms Britain is colder in the north and warmer in the south, drier in the east and wetter in the west. There are other issues such as altitude and exposure to winds, and factors such as the Gulf stream or mid-Atlantic drift. South-facing gardens get the most sun and produce earlier crops.

You can learn a lot looking around existing gardens. The nearer they are to your own home the better for comparison purposes. Excessive exposure can be cured by putting up shelter in the short term, or in the longer term by planting hedges or trees. All this costs money, however!

Check local prices of fencing, also hedging plants such as privet, thorn, beech, hornbeam, lonicera, hybrid roses. If there is room, look also at taller hedging such as Leyland cypress. Privet is quick and cheap – and roots easily from cuttings – but all hedges will require trimming. Some, like Leyland cypress, can get embarrassingly large.

Hedges have roots, and these can not only damage buildings but rob the soil of plant nutrients. They also create shade and this could be an embarrassment to yourself or a neighbour. See also Chapter 6.

TYPE OF HOUSE AND LOCAL AMENITIES

Homes vary enormously in design up and down the country, and in very general terms gardens often tend to be type-cast according to the style of house. An old cottage-type random garden adjoining a brand new home of modern design would look a little bizarre, as indeed would the reverse. Gardens often lack individuality, but designing or changing or developing a garden is something which must be approached with careful thought. Keep a strict eye to costs involved.

TREES

Buying and planting even small trees can take a hefty bite out of the gardening budget, so existing trees usually provide a welcome established feature at no extra cost. Too many tall trees, however, may mean a garden which receives little sun, and overhanging branches and vigorous roots can cause problems which, if left unresolved, may prove expensive or even dangerous. Further difficulties can arise if the troublesome trees or hedges belong to a neighbour, but do try to resolve differences amicably – lawyers' bills and unfriendly neighbours are both to be avoided at all costs.

If you fancy yourself as a lumberjack, power saws can be hired at reasonable charges, but they can be very dangerous. Felling and limbing trees can also be tricky. Large trees are best dealt with by a fully-insured, well-equipped contractor. In your efforts to save costs, you could end up with a very expensive problem if you damage buildings or persons. Before you start felling or limbing trees, check with your local authority whether a tree preservation order (TPO) is in force.

COST-SAVING SUMMARY

Levels are important. It pays to consider slope, south being ideal. The site for a new garden should preferably be clean, although you can use odd items.

The amount of top soil, and its quality, is vitally important. Sticky clay soils are difficult to work when wet, and bake hard when dry. Medium soils are easiest to work. Light soils are easy to dig, but dry out quickly and may be less fertile. Soil should be preferably free of weeds, especially bad perennial types. Drainage is vital, as a soggy garden can be a menace.

The general locality of any area and the overall effects of the weather should be kept very much in mind.

Finally, try to match the type of house you have with the type of garden proposed. Note whether large trees or hedges are likely to be a problem, and do not be over-ambitious with lopping or removal.

CHAPTER 3

THE TOOLS FOR THE JOB

It is difficult to do any serious gardening without the following basic tools and equipment (Fig. 1). Stick to necessities at the right price bracket. Look out for end-of-season stock clearances, as you can often pick up bargains. It is important to note that prices given are an average, based on summer 1991 recommended retail prices.

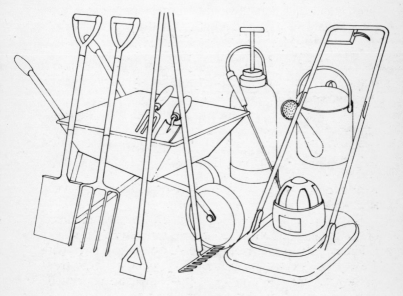

FIG 1 A range of essential garden tools.

ESSENTIAL TOOLS

Spade	Watering can
Fork	Trowel and hand fork
Wheelbarrow	Hand sprayer(s)
Rake	Lawn mower (unless no
Hoe	grass

THE ESSENTIALS

SPADES

A spade is the gardener's best friend. It is used for digging, edging, lifting turf, moving material and countless other tasks. Spades come in more than one size, including a lightweight border spade, so choose one suitable to your strength and the work it will be required to do.

Top of the range stainless steel spades last for ever but are expensive. The very cheapest spades are usually bad buys, blunting and bending easily. Go for the middle of the range. Whatever spade you choose, pick it up as you would a cricket bat, golf club or tennis racket, and see how it feels in your hands.

Price range: Supermarket 'cheapies' £10; border spade £20; stainless steel £85; stainless steel border £79.

FORKS

Forks, like spades, come in different sizes and qualities. They are essential for pricking land, forking it, moving rubbish or sometimes for digging heavy land.

The smallest fork is good for getting between shrubs and plants. Once again, see how it feels in your hands.

Price range: as for spades.

BARROWS

You can't get far without a barrow. They can be of plastic or metal and I would go for a galvanized type. Broad wheels are essential to avoid sinking into soft earth. One excellent type has a ball wheel and is not expensive.

Price range: Discounted self-assembly £19; good mid-range £35–40; galvanized £70; ball barrow £60.

RAKES

Some are made of wood, others of steel or alloy. Go for the middle of the range, a 10- or 12-tooth model being ideal. Alloy makes for easy working, with no rust. If you have a lot of raking of leaves or grass from the lawn, a springtined rake is useful and not expensive.

Price range: £10–20; stainless steel £38–40; spring-tined lawn rake £10–15.

HOES

Hoes loosen soil between trees, shrubs, and other items, chop off weeds, weed gravel paths, take out seed drills, and similar tasks. You can't really get far without a hoe. As with a spade or fork, feel is important and remember you are looking for a hoe that is functional.

Price range: Discount 'cheapies' £10; good quality Dutch £15–20; stainless steel £30.

SPRAYERS

Small hand sprays are cheap, and it is a good idea to have one for weedkillers and one for pesticides. Avoid mixing the two.

Price range: Hand misters £1; hand sprayers £7–10; lance sprayers £15–35.

ODDMENTS

You will find a trowel and a hand fork indispensable for weeding and planting. Prices range from about £2 for a cheap brand which may bend easily, to £18–20 for stainless steel, but a good quality fork and trowel should be available for about £5–7 each.

Spirit levels have many uses. Pruning saws come in handy for trimming trees or hedges – not forgetting hedge shears and secateurs. You cannot overlook watering cans, sprinkers, and a hosepipe. Avoid buying cheap plastic hoses, as they are affected by ultraviolet light. Prices vary widely. For a new garden, you will find a pick handy for loosening land, and prising out stones. This can be borrowed.

A small riddle (£2–3 for plastic; £4–5 for metal) can be invaluable when making up compost – a sound practice, as compost prices have gone up considerably in recent years. (See Chapter 4.)

Other useful items include a garden line, complete with reel and pin, although a couple of sticks and twine is almost as good. This is for defining straight lines, making paths, taking out seed drills, and other tasks demanding some precision.

Patent tools – hand cultivators, special hoes, ridgers etc. – tend to be pricey and a more basic item may do the job as well, be more versatile and cost less.

LAWN MOWERS

If you have a lawn, you will need a mower. Most suppliers have a big range to choose from, and you should not be frightened to ask for a test. It pays to compare prices.

There are two basic types of lawn mower: cylinder and rotary.

CYLINDER MOWERS

These cut the grass with blades arranged along a rotating cylinder, and move along either on a rear roller or side wheels. It is the rear roller which leaves your lawn with that nice striped appearance. Cylinders give a clean, close cut and have grassboxes to collect the grass. (The current trend is to leave the mowings lying to feed the grass. This saves time, but uncontaminated cuttings are a valuable component of the compost bin.)

Hand-push models or motorized mowers, powered by electricity or petrol, are all available. Prices for non-powered mowers vary from £40 for the cheapest side wheel cylinder, up to £69 for a 30 cm (12 in) roller mower. Small electric mowers start at around £80, petrol mowers at £290. Best buys are discontinued models.

ROTARY MOWERS

Rotary mowers, which cut the grass with circulating blades similar to a helicopter's, are superb for undulating land or dealing with odd corners, but not so good for edges, Be careful, as the whirling blades can be very dangerous. Some are self-propelled, others powered. Most collect grass. There are some excellent buys, with prices starting at around £50. New types have a rear roller to give a striped effect to the lawn.

Hover-type rotary mowers, powered either by electricity or petrol, operate on a cushion of air and are ideal for sloping or bumpy sites, and are competitively priced. Again, care is needed in their use.

WHICH TO CHOOSE?

The cylinder types give a good finish. Rotary types leave the grass longer, and don't give a striped effect unless they have a rear roller. With a small lawn, a hand-push cylinder mower may be all that is required, but for medium and larger-sized lawns, go for a self-propelled model. A good self-propelled cylinder mower will cost from £300 upwards. You can buy ride-on mowers at keen prices, but you will need a lot of grass to justify the cost.

If you buy secondhand, and buy privately, take someone who knows mowers with you. Buying from a reputable dealer, mowers are usually well-serviced and in good condition.

OTHER POWERED GADGETS

Hedge cutters can be petrol-driven but electric ones are the most popular. It is a question of scale whether it is worth buying, sharing with neighbours, or hiring. Many gardeners use cultivators in the spring to avoid digging. It is unlikely that the cost of a cultivator (from £300) would be justified; they can be hired at a reasonable price. Odd items such as mechanical hoes, strimmers, edging tools and miscellaneous mechanical items are worth investing in if you use them a lot, but, again, most can be hired at reasonable cost. It is pointless to have valuable equipment unused for 95 per cent of the year.

COLLECTIVE BUYING OF MACHINERY

It can be worth joining in with a local gardening club, allotment club or other group to buy equipment. Cultivators come into this category and a once-for-all investment of £10 or £20 could be worth while – given good maintenance, otherwise the scheme falls down.

GREENHOUSES AND FRAMES

This is about raising plants earlier and keeping them in good condition later, and growing tender plants with greater success than if they were grown entirely out of doors. But is a greenhouse really necessary, or are you simply keeping up with the Joneses? Lots can be done in the home, sowing seeds and rooting cuttings on a warm window sill, or using a patio or conservatory.

It is nice to have lettuce, tomatoes or cucumbers from your own greenhouse, but (see Chapter 8) you can possibly buy these a lot cheaper in your greengrocer or supermarket. You will, however, miss the fun of producing your own, and it takes a lot to beat freshly harvested produce.

With greenhouses, you get what you pay for. Look for strength, general stability and adequate ventilation. The cheapest greenhouses should be considered only in very sheltered situations, as they often have very basic glazing systems and flimsy structures – you may find the first gale wreaks dreadful damage. Replacing glass, or for that matter plastic, can be costly.

Up-market greenhouses are pricey, but you get substantial construction with a superior capped glazing system, which will stand up to the weather and give little bother for years. Many gardeners choose instead a conservatory attached to the home to use year round, and linked to the home heating system. Quality conservatories are not cheap either, but they can serve as an extra room and seeds, cuttings and crops like tomatoes or cucumbers can be grown in grow-bags.

Heating a greenhouse can be expensive and it is worth going carefully into the economics (Chapter 8) before committing yourself to a costly investment.

BUYING SECONDHAND GREENHOUSES

There are some first-class bargains to be picked up, provided you don't mind doing a bit of work taking down a greenhouse and re-erecting it. Many second-hand greenhouses are made of wood, but check they are of the Dutch type with dry-grooved glazing; the old putty-and-nail system cannot be advised. A lot can be done to improve even an old greenhouse by covering glazing bars with sealing tape.

PLASTIC STRUCTURES

Many gardeners interested in summer salad crops opt for cheap plastic greenhouses. It is remarkable how useful a low-cost construction of polythene and wood can be, knocked together with waste wood, with polythene or plastic secured to it by wrapping around wooden laths. Heavy-gauge polythene (around 8p per sq m or yd) is probably the best compromise, as some plastics are quite dear. The price range is £100–150.

Cloches (Fig. 2a) can be very useful as a means of protection. The latest innovation is floating mulches – perforated plastics or fleeces laid over crops to expand as the crop grows.
Price range: plastic tunnel £17 for 5 m (16 ft); floating mulch or protective fleece 35–40p per sq m (sq yd).

COLD FRAMES AND ELECTRIC PROPAGATORS

A highly efficient way of raising plants is with cold frames (Fig. 2b), either purchased or self-made with polythene and wood. Cold frames cost from £35–55 but can be built for a fraction of this. Placed in a sunny position, they are excellent for sowing seeds and raising a wide range of plants. Still more important is using them for hardening off – acclimatizing plants raised in a greenhouse or home to outside conditions.

Electric propagators (Fig. 2c) are immensely valuable, for starting off seeds or rooting cuttings. They are *very* cheap to run. Prices range from £12 to around £100.

A cheap source of localized heat is soil-warming cable on a sand-covered bench in the greenhouse (Fig. 2d). They come as a kit, with full directions. A polythene tent

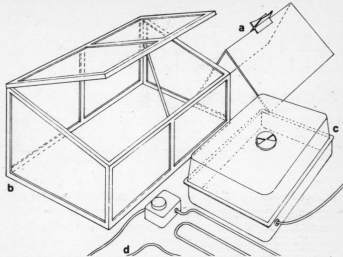

FIG 2 *A variety of methods available to protect or nurture young plants or seedlings: (a) cloche; (b) cold frame; (c) electric propagator; (d) soil-warming cable.*

over the bench will conserve heat, but humidity levels can be high. The cable costs around £1 per 30 cm/ft and a thermostat £35–40.

SHEDS

For somewhere to keep all your tools and equipment try a sectional shed or a glass-fronted potting shed. This is excellent for limited plant-raising. Compare quality and prices at a display centre.

COST-SAVING SUMMARY

Spend your money wisely after deciding you really need something. Don't buy expensive items which will be used for a brief period and then left doing nothing. This applies to greenhouses, too. Consider hiring, or collective buying. Shop around for secondhand bargains.

CHAPTER 4

FERTILE SOILS, WITHOUT WASTE

Plants take in food by absorbing gases through their leaves and literally sucking up solutions of plant foods, mainly through their roots. These elements are prepared or 'cooked' by the countless millions of micro-organisms which live in soils and many composts. Some plant foods can be absorbed directly.

PLANT FOODS

Plants absorb their food in simple element form, and each performs a different basic function:

Nitrogen (N): largely concerned with leaf growth. High nitrogen feeds are ideal for salads.

Phosphorus (P): good root development largely depends on adequate levels of phosphorus.

Potassium (K): concerned with quality and colour of flowering plants. Particularly useful for plants such as tomatoes.

It is often a question of balance – nitrogen inducing soft, leafy growth, and potassium balancing or hardening growth.

Calcium, referred to as lime, is important for keeping a soil sweet. The measure of lime present or absent is the pH scale, with figures between 5 and 7 as normal. It pays to check that soils are adequately supplied with lime, using a testing kit which will cost as little as 50p.

Elements such as magnesium, manganese and others are usually available to plants in sufficient quantities. Many complete fertilizers and organic manures contain a range of minor elements.

THE IMPORTANCE OF HUMUS

A soil well-endowed with micro-organisms, with plenty of work for them to do, is said to be fertile. The decomposition of organic matter provides humus. This gums small particles together, creating aeration and drainage channels. Humus also acts as an absorbent sponge for moisture and plant nutrients, and encourages microbiological activity. There has to be good drainage and adequate rainfall, or artificial watering. What foods the plants do not absorb will be washed into the drains, so it is common sense *not to overfeed*.

Fertility of soils is not something which just happens. You have to put in a bit of effort to achieving it and maintaining it. It costs money. There should be a happy balance between bulky materials to improve the physical structure of soil, provide vital humus and plant foods, along with the sensible use of more concentrated fertilizers.

CHECKING THE FERTILITY OF YOUR SOIL

This can be done by sending away a soil sample for analysis, for which a charge is generally made. You can do it more quickly and cheaply by buying a soil testing kit. This will tell you the levels of the main elements, including lime. More importantly, it will give guidance on whether you need to apply nutrients and in what quantities.

Organic enthusiasts use organic manures and organically-based fertilizers only, along with compost. Plant foods provided in this way are not so prone to being flushed out of the soil, but are generally more expensive.

MAKING COMPOST

A major source of organic material is properly prepared compost. This comes from the rotting down of organic refuse, such as grass cuttings, leaves of vegetables, stems, and soft household waste. An electric shredder can grind down hard material. The ideal is a mix of soft and harder material.

There are various methods of composting, and different compost-makers available. Basically, it involves stacking materials, ideally of a similar stage of decomposition, into bins or trenches. Polythene sheets over compost heaps protect them from excessive moisture, but a vital ingredient for successful compost is air, through the base and sides of the heap. Compost activators, costing from around £2 upwards, help the natural breaking-down process, especially in a smaller heap. For further details on constructing a compost heap, refer to a companion volume in this series, *The Environmentally Friendly Garden*.

ORGANIC MANURES

Organic manures have various sources, and you must evaluate what they achieve in improving soil fertility and providing nutrients. The average bag of poultry-derived manure, containing 15–25 kg (35–55 lb) and costing £5–9 is claimed to dress around 100 sq m (120 sq yd), so the cost is not high.

Ideally, organic manures should be bought in bulk, making considerable savings. There are other materials such as seaweed, and you can buy various forms which are effective for soil conditioning and supplying plant nutrients. They tend to be more expensive.

GREEN MANURING

This excellent and cost-effective way of improving soil texture adds organic matter and supplies plant food. It involves sowing out various fast-growing plants at differing times which, when grown, can be dug back into the soil. It is recommended that many of these green manures be cut over, to avoid seeding before cultivating them into the soil.

SOME POPULAR MANURES OR FERTILIZERS

Type	Comments	N%	P%	K%
* horse manure	Well balanced, usually quite cheap if collected at riding schools	0.7	0.3	0.6
* cow manure	Inclined to be rather sticky and wet	0.6	0.2	.5
* pig manure	Like cow manure can be very unpleasant unless well composted, usually cheap	0.6	0.3	0.05
* goat manure	Usually available free from goat farms	1.4	0.2	1.0
* hen-derived manures	Very variable, should not be used raw, can be high in nitrogen. The best are well composted and sterilized. There are several brands on the market. Best to buy in bulk through groups.	1.3–3	1.5	variable
rabbit manure	Can be available in quantity if you are near a rabbit farm	2.4	1.4	variable
pigeon manure	Like rabbit manure often freely available but can be very 'hot' (high in nitrogen)	5.0	2.4	2.3
bone meal (organic)	Useful, expensive slow-acting fertilizer	5.0	20.0	nil
dried blood (organic)	Safe boosting fertilizer, expensive	10–12	nil	nil
fish manure	Variable, excellent source of nutrients	10.0	8.0	7.0

Type	Comments	N%	P%	K%
hoof and horn meal (organic)	Safe but expensive	12–14	nil	nil
seaweed	Extremely variable, usually rich in trace elements and has other assets	5.0	mini-mal	1.5
sulphate of potash (inorganic)	Quick source of potash	nil	nil	50.0
superphos-phates (inorganic)	Best source of phosphates	nil	15–18	nil
sulphate of ammonia (inorganic)	Quick-acting, use with care, useful for compost making	20.0	nil	nil
lime	Essential to keep soil sweet, except in limestone areas	Variable levels of calcium		
Growmore	Balanced, cheap and effective	7	7	7
spent hops and spent mush-room compost	More readily available in some areas than others: excellent for improving soil or mulching, can be very cheap	analysis very variable		
municipal compost	Starting to be available again, more will come on market as methods of refuse disposal change	Always variable, can be problems of heavy metals		

* Analysis of organic manures can vary considerably. It is essential to follow the instructions given.

With materials such as sewage sludge, spent hops, brewery and distillery waste, and composted straw, analysis and price obviously vary. Many are lately on the market. There are also compound fertilizers, some organically-based, others a mixture of organic and inorganic, some entirely inorganic. Many compound fertilizers contain a range of trace elements and are useful.

Prices of fertilizers vary from 80p per kg (2 lb) (Growmore) up to £2.50 for the same weight of sophisticated types. Lime is around 40p per kg (2 lb).

The analysis of all proprietary fertilizers is stated

clearly on the bag or packet: nitrogen (N) first, phosphate (P) second, and potassium or potash (K) third. The analysis of other elements is not always given.

GROWING COMPOSTS

There are many growing composts, ranging from seed-sowing types through to long-term growing composts. You can mix your own at about 50–60 per cent of the cost of buying. Collective purchase of these bulk items can save up to 40 per cent of recommended retail prices. Despite the environmental lobby, peat-based composts are very popular, and this is likely to be the position for some time ahead. They cost around 10–12p per litre.

Soil-based composts of the John Innes formulae are generally slightly dearer than peat composts, at 12–13p per litre.

MIXING YOUR OWN COMPOSTS

The problem with any soil-based compost is finding clean, reliable soil free from pests, diseases and weeds, with the right physical characteristics. Soil can be sterilized, and the most reliable soil is usually from wasteland or land that has been uncropped for many years.

The formulae for John Innes soil-based composts are as follows:

Note: 1 bushel = 36 litres = 8 gallons = 4 × 2 gallons or bushel apple box

For seed growing

2 parts (by bulk) loam (good soil), ideally sterilized
1 part (by bulk) peat (good quality, good texture)
1 part (by bulk) sharp sand or fine gravel (or Perlite or vermiculite at recommended rates)

To each bushel of this mix, allowing 15–20 per cent

shrinkage, add:
42 g (1½ oz) superphosphates
21 g (¾ oz) ground limestone
or a proprietary slow-release fertilizer (see Note below).

For potting
John Innes No. 1 mix (suitable for potting most bedding plants and vegetables)
7 parts (by bulk) loam
3 parts (by bulk) peat
2 parts (by bulk) sand or gravel (Perlite or vermiculite)
To each bushel of this mix (allowing 15–20 per cent shrinkage) add 112 g (4 oz) John Innes base, i.e.:
2 parts (by weight) hoof and horn meal
2 parts (by weight) superphosphates
1 part (by weight) sulphate of potash
21 g (¾ oz) ground limestone

John Innes No.2 (for growing plants or for ring culture of tomatoes)
Double quantities of fertilizer and lime, i.e.: 224 g (8 oz) John Innes base and 42 g (1.5 oz) ground limestone

John Innes No.3 (for growing plants long term. Can be used for tomatoes, but risky)
Treble quantities of fertilizer and lime, i.e.: 335 g (12 oz) John Innes base and 63 g (2¼ oz) ground limestone

Note: Many gardeners now prefer a complete base fertilizer such as Vitax Q4, Osmocote or Chempak (separate lime *is not needed*) or other bases used according to directions. Prices are around £1.45 for base to mix 100 litres of compost.

PEAT-BASED COMPOSTS

It is quite simple to mix up your own compost using one of the special compost base fertilizers available. It will cost around £1.45 for enough base to mix 100 litres of compost, and the cost of 100 litres of peat is around £6, so compost will cost around 7–8p per litre. Always mix on a clean floor, where there is no risk of weedkiller, and mix thoroughly.

COST-SAVING SUMMARY

Buy organic manures and fertilizers in as large a quantity as you can justify. Before applying any organic manures or fertilizers, measure up your land carefully and calculate what you need. A useful preliminary is to test soils or have the soil analysed.

CHAPTER 4

A GARDEN FRAMEWORK

Although it is usually the plants, especially the flowers, which excite most interest in a garden, it is worth planning with care the 'hard' elements which are going to provide the basic framework to the garden: the paths and patios as well as permanent features such as pergolas and rockeries. Also included in this category, although most definitely living, is one of the most common elements in garden design: the lawn.

LAWNS

Lawns are the most popular long-term gardening feature: low-cost to develop and relatively easy to maintain. They do, nevertheless, involve constant cutting and money must be spent on mowers, plant foods and moss control on a fairly regular basis.

There are two basic ways of making a lawn: from seed and from turf. Preparation of the ground is the same: ensure there are no drainage problems; thoroughly dig over the area, raking and firming to provide a stone-free, well-consolidated surface.

Ground prepared in spring can be hoed regularly or treated with *contact* weed killer, for sowing in autumn. Alternatively, ground can be left over winter for weeds to develop before being treated. Immediately prior to sowing, get a nice even tilth by raking. When turfing, a layer of sharp sand provides a level surface.

SEEDING

For the highly decorative show lawn invest in the best dwarf lawn grasses. For an all-purpose lawn, go for a medium quality mixture. For rough grass areas, cheaper mixtures will do; these usually contain perennial rye grass. For under trees, there are special shade mixtures.

Scatter on a good general fertilizer at around 68 g per sq m (2 oz per sq yd) and rake it in thoroughly. Then sow seed around 34 g per sq m (1 oz per sq yd), raking in lightly. To help with even distribution, the ground can be marked off into strips with white string.

TURFING

For turfing the same preparatory procedures are followed. Turf is available in various qualities, from field turf which will withstand children's games to the finest quality for golf, putting and bowling greens. Obviously select the type most appropriate to your needs. Much of the price of turf is in transport, and it can be a lot cheaper if you collect it.

Lay turf evenly, standing or kneeling on a broad board. Stagger the joints as with a brick wall. It may be beaten down lightly with the back of a spade, and given a top dressing of sand or sandy soil worked in to the cracks.

COSTS

The cost of seed averages around £3.50 per kilo which at average sowing rates will cost about 10p per sq m or sq yd. Turf, on the other hand, can cost from £1–2.50 per sq yd (it is still sold by the sq yd). Fertilizer is around 80p–£1 kg or 3p per sq m (sq yd).

SUBSEQUENT TREATMENT

Avoid drying out, especially when turfing. Seed germinates in 14–21 days and should be cut when 5–6 cm (2–3 in) tall. Avoid tugging the young grass out of the ground. Turf usually develops quickly and should be cut lightly. A light rolling is beneficial after a week or so.

ANNUAL TREATMENT

The most effective way of keeping a lawn in trim is cutting. Unless lawns are very level, very close cutting is not advised since this can cause skinning on high places, which may encourage moss. A common sense approach is advisable. Cut a decorative lawn about twice a week, from late spring until September or October. In hot, dry weather, frequent cutting is not advised unless the lawn is watered regularly.

Many gardeners maintain that decomposing mowings help to feed the grass. This is fine if the grass is cut regularly. Otherwise, it can create problems of weed and moss encouragement. Other gardeners prefer to collect mowings in the grass-box. Experiment and decide what suits your lawn best.

Effective maintenance of edges is a constant problem. Edging shears are usual, although wheeled cutters are quicker. An edging tool, while useful, is not essential, as a sharp garden spade will trim edges almost as well.

Feed lawns in the spring, making sure application is even. Special lawn fertilizers are less liable to scorch. Top dressing with sand or compost improves levels, applied in early autumn or spring. With no restrictions, regular watering in hot weather avoids the grass browning.

Slitting or spiking aerates the surface and improves drainage. A reasonably good job can be done with a garden fork or a hand-piercer, although it is laborious and time-consuming. Hollow tining with a special fork takes out cores of soil and should be followed by top dressing brushed into the holes. Specialized equipment such as slitters, spikers and scarifiers can be hired.

LAWN TROUBLES

One of the main problems is moss, dealt with by moss-killing chemicals. The cheapest way is to mix up sulphate of iron and sulphate of ammonia, with sand to facilitate spreading. Take 20 parts of sand to 3 parts of sulphate of ammonia and 1 part sulphate of iron (parts by weight), applied at around 68 g per sq m (2 oz per sq yd). It can be bought at around £1.90 per 3 kg as lawn sand. Combined proprietary moss-killers/fertilizers tend to be costly in comparison, but are very effective. Moss killing is best done in early spring, *before scarifying or raking out*. If the lawn is raked with living moss in it, the problem will simply be spread around.

Weeds can be dealt with by hormone-type weed-killers, although lawn sand mixture also controls weeds to an extent.

Various diseases can also attack lawns; seek advice at your local garden centre. Some diseases such as rust can be difficult to control and you are often wasting money trying to combat them.

HARD GARDENS

When the weather is fine our inclination is to enjoy it to the full and live out of doors as much as possible. Barbecues, garden furniture, patios and terraces all increase our enjoyment of outdoor living. The other reason why hard patios and gravelled recreational areas have become so universally popular is that, although somewhat expensive to construct at the outset, hard gardens demand little in the way of maintenance, and so can be a good long-term investment. In broad essence, they involve slabbing, walling, bricks, gravel, concrete, asphalt and synthetic surfaces generally.

Soil is of little account as most of it is going to be covered anyway, apart from planting through gravelled areas. What is important is good drainage and freedom from bad perennial weeds, and even weeds are not an insurmountable problem as they can generally be dealt with on a localized basis.

Hard garden areas are usually flat or nearly so. Although this is not an absolute necessity, it is desirable, since a definite slope can mean quite a bit of levelling, terracing or other heavy reconstructional work.

A PLAN OF CAMPAIGN

It is essential to sketch out exactly what you are planning to do. Glean ideas from books, articles, other people's gardens, visits to display garden centres, flower shows, indeed anywhere where you can gain inspiration. Before setting to work, some measuring is also desirable, ending up with a reasonably accurate scale drawing. There may be those who can work to eye, or by guesswork, but this generally tends to be unsatisfactory as it is almost impossible to calculate for the necessary materials. Many garden centres stock a range of material, and there are DIY building yards up and down the country. Double check when buying that you get sufficient for your needs. It should be possible, with a scale plan and a little research into local prices, to come to a fairly accurate estimate of costs.

GETTING DOWN TO CONSTRUCTION

Getting in a landscaper to undertake all the work for you would be the most expensive way of going about things. If one has sights on a landscaped garden but not the time, ability or inclination to get on with construction,

BUILDING MATERIALS (Average prices, 1991, excluding VAT)

The following is a typical list, with prices and quantities for the average range of material used in creating a hard garden. Prices will vary around the country and with the passage of time. There may be a quantity discount available.

Materials	Per bag (50 kg)	Per tonne
Washed building sand	78p	£8.95
Washed concrete sand	90p	£9.95
5 mm–20 mm gravel	90p	£10.00
20 mm quartz gravel	£1.10	£16.00
14 mm red whin chips	£1.25	£16.60
144 mm granite chips	£1.40	£21.50
Whin dust	80p	£9.50

Gravel covers approximately 1 sq m/sq yd per bag.

Hydraulic pressed paving	Grey	Coloured
600 × 300 × 50 mm	£1.20	
600 × 450 × 50 mm	£1.76	
600 × 600 × 50 mm	£1.76	£2.60
900 × 600 × 50 mm	£2.50	£3.30

Hydraulic pressed edging	Grey	Colour
900 × 150 × 50 mm	£1.25	–
900 × 200 × 50 mm	£1.55	–
900 × 250 × 50 mm	£2.00	–

finding or borrowing the money for a professional layout is at least a practical answer.

If undertaking the work yourself, tools required for construction are minimal: a spade, shovel, pick, barrow, a trowel for spreading cement, a spirit level and straight boards, with the occasional hire of cement mixers if doing an extensive amount of mixing or building work.

There is no overall yardstick for constructional techniques. It is better to take one feature at a time. Hasty construction is never advised, especially where a lot of soil movement is involved as there is bound to be consolidation and subsidence. This is especially true of walls. It is vital to have a firm base and level surface for all slabbing or walling activities. Slabs can be laid on a dry mix of three parts sand to one of cement, which hardens in time.

Spreading gravel does not demand such meticulous preparation. There are some delightful gardens these days which are a mixture of slabs, walls and gravels. A gravel mulch is often best combined with small specimen trees.

WOOD IN THE GARDEN

Wood has always been a popular choice for garden constructions in the garden, and in the 1990s is becoming more so. Wood and products such as wood bark have exceptional qualities for blending in with most types of gardens, whether used for fencing, furniture, paths or garden buildings.

Many gardeners have greenhouses and frames made of wood (Chapter 3), and here again prices are competitive. Rustic wood for making pergolas and arches, with bark or without and varnished, can transform a flat and uninteresting garden into a delightful area, especially when clothed with climbing roses or shrubs. A visit to your local sawmill or DIY centre can confirm prices.

In terms of cost, wood-derived furniture and basic wood for construction has in recent years tended to become very competitive. It is usually quite easy to cost out any particular project, following planning and measurement for interwoven fencing, seats, tables, benches and the like. These can be costed according to requirements.

LASTING QUALITIES OF WOOD

Above ground, untreated wood in rustic form can last for a considerable period, much depending on climate. Bark will be retained for 10–12 yeaars, the wood lasting for 20 years or more. Varnished pressure-treated or creosoted wood should last much longer, especially when regularly treated with preservatives.

Below ground, wood of any kind will deteriorate rapidly if exposed to cold and damp. There is much to be said for using cement piles to insulate wood from cold and damp. This can be achieved by using old metal buckets or cans filled with concrete, or large diameter drainage pipes filled with sand and bitumen.

Less long-lasting but reasonably effective is to secure

COMPARATIVE COSTS OF COMMONLY AVAILABLE WOODEN PANELS AND TRELLISING. (Prices excluding VAT.)

Interwoven panels	1.8 × 1.8 m (6 × 6 ft)	£12–13
	1.8 × 1.5 m (6 × 5 ft)	£11–12
	1.8 × 1.2 m (6 × 4 ft)	£10–11
Overlap panels	1.8 × 1.8 m (6 × 6 ft)	£13–14
	1.8 × 1.5 m (6 × 5 ft)	£12–13
	1.8 × 1.2 m (6 × 4 ft)	£11–12
Wooden square trellis	1.8 m × 30 cm (6 × 1 ft)	£4.50–5
	1.8 m × 60 cm (6 × 2 ft)	£7.50–8
	1.8 m × 90 cm (6 × 3 ft)	£10–11
	1.8 × 1.2 m (6 × 4 ft)	£14–14.50
Lattice border	90 × 30 cm (3 × 1 ft)	around £7
Expanding trellis	1.8 × 1.2 m (6 × 4 ft)	£20–21

For other wooden items, check out your local sawmill or DIY outlet.

the base of any section of wood on a portion of concrete slab and surround it with broken bricks.

Bark mulches set off a 'wooden garden' theme, costing around £8–9 per 80-litre bag, or a lot cheaper bought in bulk. Log rolls set off beds superbly. These are usually available in two heights, 15 cm (6 in) or 30 cm (12 in) and cost around £5–9 for a metre length.

Wood garden furniture is available in huge variety at DIY and garden centres. It pays to shop around. On the other hand, the handyman can make a lot of furniture using spare wood at very little cost.

ROCK GARDENS AND SCREES

Rock gardens have the reputation of being expensive and indeed they can be if costly ornamental stone is selected. But if a source of demolished sandstone or local quarrystone can be tracked down, the price need not be high. An average price for stone around the country is around £15 per ton but for superior stone such as weather-worn Westmoreland the price is considerably higher. Here again, it pays to check around landscape supply depots.

ROCKERIES ARE NOT HEAPS OF STONES

A common mistake when constructing a rockery is not to imitate natural rock strata (Fig. 3). This is the way in which the shelves of rock run in a specific direction. Have a look around at various rockeries to get your ideas right.

The site for the rockery should be free of bad perennial weeds. Drainage should also be reasonably good, although by constructing a rock garden one is, in a way, developing a different type of drainage system. Rock gardens need by no means be confined to sloping sites – they can make superb raised features.

bad

good

FIG 3 Good and bad examples of stones laid to form a rock garden. As in nature, the strata should all run the same way and the major part of each rock should be buried by soil.

The basic objective is to bury about three-quarters of the stone under the surface and create lots of attractive pockets for plants to grow. In addition, you will require appreciable quantities of well-drained gritty soil. Alternatively, good quality soil will be needed. Plan your rock garden carefully and be prepared for one or two false starts. An artistic eye helps enormously.

SCREE

Scree beds are ideal for sloping sites. They are constructed with a deep layer of gravel or stone of various sizes on an area which has been cleared of all growth (which may mean lifting turf or killing off grass). Like a conventional rock garden, a scree bed provides the perfect conditions for alpines and other plants which require good drainage.

PLANTS FOR ROCK GARDENS

There is an infinite range of suitable plants. Many are readily produced from seeds or cuttings. Membership of a horticultural society or your local rock garden group should provide a rich source of material. Gardeners often have surplus material which they are happy to get rid of.

Occasional top dressing with peat or good compost is a sound idea with most rockeries, particularly after they have subsided somewhat, or in wet areas where there may be some degree of erosion.

A few of the more popular rock garden plants (average cost £1–1.50 from a garden centre) are: alyssum, arabis, armeria, aubrieta, draba, gentian, iberis (candytuft), lewisia, dwarf phlox, saxifrage, sedum, sempervivum, thyme.

PEAT WALL GARDENS

Block peat is not always easy to obtain, but can provide an exceedingly attractive peat garden, with an ideal environment for acid-loving plants. The objective is to build raised beds, in the same way as one would use walling stone. The beds or raised areas created are filled with one of the blacker and cheaper peats, or sandy soil.

A peat wall garden makes an ideal haven for a range of heathers, rhododendrons, azaleas, and some of the more interesting and colourful plants such as meconopsis.

COST-SAVING SUMMARY

Check out the local newspaper for special offers in the classified section. For rockery stone a visit to a demolition yard could be worthwhile. Visit smaller specialist nurseries to obtain rockery plants – they will be much cheaper than in larger garden centres.

CHAPTER 5

SHRUBS, HEDGES AND TREES

It takes a lot to beat shrubs and trees as long-term features. Their low initial cost and the pleasure they give over many years goes with their versatility in different soil types and locations.

You don't need to rush out and buy a big mass of shrubs or trees. Do this gradually over a period as money is available. This gives you time to shop around and compare prices. If you can wait a little longer for results, many shrubs or trees are simple to raise from seeds, cuttings or layers. Many indeed are spread around gardens by birds or wind, and you can find seedlings for free in all sorts of odd corners.

There is considerable merit in choosing shrubs or trees you know do well in your area, which can be established with a walk around. You may feel you want something a little different, but check that the specimens you have your eye on are going to thrive in your particular garden, or your money and care may be wasted.

PLANNING AND PLANTING

Shrubs and trees are attractive at different times of year, not only in terms of flower but of stems and foliage. Have a mix of flowering times, with some evergreens to give year-round colour. Get out a few catalogues or books and walk around garden centres to get an idea of the different effects and combinations.

Shrubs are usually grouped into borders, although some lend themselves to specimen planting. The same is true of trees. Plan to put shrubs and trees where they will best provide colour and effect. They may also serve for shelter or privacy. Many shrubs and particularly trees can develop to a large size, so choose the right specimens for the right position.

Draw a sketch plan, numbering the position for various shrubs and trees, noting that trees should not become an embarrassment in the years to come because you have under-estimated the size to which they will grow.

A common mistake is to plant quick-growing shrubs too closely together: in a year or two drastic thinning is necessary. This is a waste of money. Climbing shrubs are excellent for masking unpleasant features such as walls or buildings, and the same is true of taller shrubs and trees. Planting for immediate effect is obviously going to cost you more, so check on the particular growth habits of any shrub or tree you choose. Planting distances range from 30 cm (12 in) apart for heathers and similar low-growing types, to about 1.5 m (5 ft) or more for berberis and other broad shrubs. Hedge plants are usually placed about 30–45 cm (12–18 in) apart. You can buy young shrubs more cheaply than larger specimens. Mail order offers are useful, but you only get what you pay for!

PLANTING AND SOIL PREPARATION

Check that you have no obnoxious weeds such as couch grass, Japanese bamboo, or other bad perennials. If you have, you will need to consider clearance over a period of cultivation or treatment with special weed killers. In a very weedy situation, it might be better to forget shrubs and trees and put that area down to grass, or a hard surface such as paving.

Good general cultivation is advisable and if the soil is very heavy some gritty material such as sand is very helpful. On the other hand, should the soil be light and sandy it is worth digging in some clean organic matter.

The majority of shrubs or trees available from garden centres are container-grown, allowing you to plant at any time. Check that you are not getting root-bound container specimens, or those which are not well established. The former may be difficult to establish, whereas the latter can often receive a planting check when taken out of their containers.

You can buy bare root shrubs, usually a lot cheaper direct from a nursery, through mail order and from other sources but this entails planting in the autumn or the early spring.

For all planting, take out generous holes and plant at the right depth, looking for the old soil mark on the plant's stem. Plant firmly without compacting the soil. Localized soil improvement, using compost, leaf mould, or organic manure is invariably of benefit. Avoid drying out after planting. Mulching with low-cost organic materials, if available, can be very useful not only to control weeds but to conserve moisture.

CULTURAL ROUTINE

Pruning of particular types of shrubs depends on their habit of growth. Shrubs flowering later in the season are generally pruned in the early spring and spring-flowering shrubs trimmed up after flowering. Many shrubs, particularly the more common types, are not really too fussy and can be trimmed as and when required.

RAISING YOUR OWN TREES AND SHRUBS

Collecting seed heads or seed pods is an interesting and economic way of raising many trees and shrubs. Germination, often slow, comes about under relatively cool conditions in well-prepared lighter types of soil, ideally in a cold frame where there is protection from the worst elements. Some seeds even require a period of cold exposure (stratification) before germination will commence. Many shrubs can be propagated from soft cuttings taken in June or July, and hardwood cuttings taken in the autumn months. They can be rooted in sandy soils, with the help of hormone rooting power.

Propagation of shrubs and trees tends to be a specialist subject. Refer to various books on the subject for precise information on the best methods. A little time and trouble can save a considerable sum of money provided you are not looking for immediate results.

SUPPORT

Climbing shrubs will obviously be planted against some form of support. Those which are not self-clinging species will require wires, wall nails or vine eyes to support them. Trees of standard types will initially require staking, and it is vital not to use tight ties between the stem and the stake. Special expanding ties are advised.

SELECTION OF SHRUBS AND TREES

It is not possible to give a detailed list of shrubs, but here are a few suggestions of good value plants. Prices are typical of those in well-stocked garden centres and are frequently cheaper at garden nurseries or through mail order.

SHRUBS, HEDGES AND TREES

HEDGE PLANTS

Beech, box, cotoneaster, shrubby honeysuckle, Leyland cypress, privet, shrub roses, thorn, yew (slow). All except honeysuckle and box can grow tall quickly, if not trimmed. Hedging plants cost on average £1–2.50 depending on variety, size and quantity (Leyland cypress £3–4, but can be a lot cheaper by mail order).

SOME VERY RELIABLE SHRUBS

Berberis, broom, flowering currant, elder, escallonia, heather, hebe, potentilla, skimmia, spiraea, vinca.

These are all in the cheaper bracket: small ground cover shrubs such as vinca and heather may only cost £1–2; for others expect to pay around £4–7.50.

TREES

Because of the initial higher cost and comparatively slow rate of maturity, it is worth investing a little research into trees suitable for your garden. However much you may admire oak trees, an oak is not the tree for you, for example, if you have a small plot and plan to move on in a few years' time. You will have seen your tree only as a slender sapling and will be leaving a problem for your successors in twenty or thirty years! However a few carefully chosen trees can quickly add maturity to any garden.

A stroll round other people's gardens, and local gardens open to the public, should provide plenty of food for thought, but as a starting point the following are reliable and rewarding: rowans (especially for their autumn colour and berries), the many types of flowering cherries, the crab apple (for spring colour and the bonus of fruit for jam making later in the season), the weeping birch (*Betula pendula* 'Youngii') – a favourite as a focal point in a lawn.

Trees must be selected with care and well positioned to have maximum effect. Try to choose varieties that have year-round interest, be it with spring blossom, foliage colour or autumn fruits. Do take care that the particular tree you select will not outgrow its site and cause problems of root drainage to buildings or obscuring light.

ROSES

Roses range in habit from ground creepers and miniature bushes just a foot or so high, to large thorny shrubs and climbers, and ramblers which can cover a wall. Their popularity as garden plants waxes and wanes as gardeners are put off by mildew and black spot or complicated pruning techniques, or recharged with enthusiasm for a new variety or the sheer beauty and heady fragrance of a rose bush in full flower.

Roses, chosen with care and given satisfactory growing conditions, give a magnificent long-term display and are an excellent investment at around £2.75–£3.50 for container-grown bushes or £1.75–£2.75 for bare root plants. With so many varieties to choose from, there is not room here to list even a few individual recommendations, but the following points are worth bearing in mind when considering garden worthiness and value for money: disease resistance; continuous or repeat flowering habit (many of the old roses, albeit some of the most beautiful, flower only once for a few weeks in the summer); the bonus of a sweet scent and/or autumn hips; eventual size (modern 'patio' roses are now bred especially with the small garden in mind).

With a rose bed lasting for some ten years or more, it is worth preparing the soil well by digging in plenty of well-rotted farmyard manure, liming if necessary and mulching the newly planted area to help conserve moisture and discourage weeds.

It is also worth mastering the basic principles of pruning. These are not difficult and, particularly in the case of large-flowered roses, correct pruning will reward with a fine display the following year.

COST-SAVING SUMMARY

Take the time to visit several suppliers and compare prices and quality of plant specimens, checking that plants are not pot-bound or damaged in any way.

If creating an immediate effect is not the most important consideration, opt for younger specimens of trees and shrubs. These will be easier to establish and you will save a lot of money.

CHAPTER 7

BEDDING DISPLAYS AND PERENNIAL FLOWERS

ANNUALS AND BIENNIALS FOR BEDDING

Quick and easy to grow, annuals and biennials provide a mass of welcome colour for many months of the year. As well as their useful role as temporary 'fillers' in borders which have yet to establish themselves, they make a wonderful spring and summer display in their own beds.

Ideally, beds should be well drained, weed-free, with clean organic matter included. Soils should be reasonably sweet (pH 6–7). Use a balanced general fertilizer at 70 g per sq m (2 oz per sq yd). For autumn, a slow-acting organically based fertilizer such as bonemeal is valuable. (See Chapter 4 for costs of fertilizers.)

RAISING PLANTS

Self-raising plants or buying in? Not an easy decision. Do a check on costs of trays, compost, seed and heat. You may be surprised how things mount up. On the other hand, you will pay 8–10p each for plants, perhaps three or four times this for pot-grown geraniums or begonias. So sowing seed is often the easiest and cheapest way if you have more than a few tubs or baskets to plant up. At around 50p to £1, a packet of seed contains ample seed to suit most gardeners.

Germination is fairly rapid, and helped by putting seed pans or trays into polythene bags beside a hot water tank or other suitable warm place. After germination, the pots or containers go into lighter conditions, shaded from the sun until they establish themselves. Raising plants is simple with compartmentalised trays, and it is possible to sow individually or in twos or threes, thinned down when large enough to handle. Putting dabs of honey on sheets of soft paper to which seeds adhere is a cheap way of space sowing.

Propagating cases, heated greenhouses or conservatories, or even a light windowsill can all be used to raise early seedlings, but avoid sowing too early or you will end up with tender, floppy plants. For spring bedding, sow in May and June in cold frames or under cloches, bringing the plants on in a sunny border. Pansies are usually sown outdoors from June to August or under glass in March, hardening off plants to stand the winter. Similarly, biennials such as wallflowers and foxgloves are sown during the summer and planted out the following spring.

PLANTING OUT

Beds should be raked level, following cultivation. Unless a bed is very large, planting by eye is satisfactory. Plant firmly and water in if the weather has been dry. Bedding plants on the whole are resistant to pests and diseases, although slugs can be a nuisance early on. Weeds can be a hazard. With well prepared ground, supplementary feeding is not generally required, but light soils may benefit.

Planting for summer bedding is usually from late April to May or June. It can be costly to lose tender plants, which readily succumb to a late frost. It is usual to have taller items in the centre and dwarf plants for edges. Spacing varies between 20 cm (8 in) to 30 cm

(12 in) each way, which means you will need 10 or 12
plants per sq m (sq yd).

20 GOOD SUMMER BEDDING PLANTS

Plant	Location in bed	Colours	Comments
Ageratum	Edging	blue shades	Excellent edging plant, often overlooked
Alyssum	Edging	white and pink	Reliable edging plant, tends to lose flowers mid-season, better varieties awaited
Antirrhinum	Generally centre	wide range	Dwarfer types popular, seed heads can be off-putting
Aster*	Centre	wide range	Attractive but not in the top ten
Begonia†	Centre or mass	pink, red and white	Ideal for mass colour, does well in wet season
Burning Bush (Kochia)	Centre-piece	autumn foliage	Something different for marvellous effect
Busy Lizzie (Impatiens)*†	Centre for mass display	many	Truly excellent for display, superb container plant
Cabbage (ornamental)	Centre or near	coloured foliage	Something different
Carnation	Centre	pinks, reds and white	Inclined to flop, but provides plenty of cut flowers
Cosmos	Centre	wide range	Very attractive, not yet fully appreciated
Dahlia†	Centre	many	Sure display, tubers can be saved for following year

Echium	Edging	blues, pinks and white	Overlooked as bedding plant but very reliable
Fuchsia*†	Ideal in centre, especially standards	many	Becoming very popular, can be saved from year to year
Geranium*† (*Pelargonium*)	Excellent, *pièce de resistance* of bedding plants	constantly increasing range, including multi-flower types	Very much the 'in plant', thrives in sunny weather, seed heads not too pretty. Generally raised from seeds but old faithful varieties of zonal pelargoniums from cuttings still popular
Lobelia*	Edging	blues, pinks and white	Ideal edgers and trailing types, good for containers
Marigold	Edging/ centre	excellent range	Becoming more popular annually
Nemesia	Edging	pink, reds and white	Tremendous splash of early colour, tends to go off, so should not be totally relied on
Petunia*	Generally used for centre	striking colours	Can be shy of flowering in too rich soil
Salvia	Centre	shades of scarlet	Was popular and becoming more so once again
Tobacco Plant (*Nicotiana*)	Centre-piece	pinks, white, yellows	Dwarfer forms are gaining in popularity, more or less continuous flowering

* Ideal for containers
† Readily propagated from cuttings

Preparing spring bedding is similar to summer bedding. Good drainage is important, particularly in wet districts. The range of plants for spring bedding increases all the time. Bulbs, particularly tulips, are a mainstay. Wallflowers remain the most popular spring bedding plant, but are fast being overtaken by Universal pansies. Complementary planting with polyanthus, primulas, double daisies, forget-me-nots and saponarias gives a colourful result. Spacing is the same as for summer bedding.

PROPAGATING TO SAVE MONEY

Money can be saved by keeping surplus seed. Many summer bedding plants – including geraniums, begonias and busy lizzies – are half hardy perennials which can be wintered under frost-free conditions rather than discarded at the end of the season. Cuttings can be readily rooted in warmth, while spring bedding plants such as double daisies, polyanthus and primroses lend themselves to division.

CONTAINERS

An ever-increasing range of pots, tubs and baskets is available, and books and garden centres are full of imaginative ideas on how to use them. A little imagination, too, in the choice of container can save money (Fig. 4). Hanging baskets vary from reservoir types at around £2 to wire baskets at £4. Balcony planters and window box prices vary greatly. But old tyres with one edge curled up, old sinks, barrows or other items all make suitable plant holders. A handyman can often make window boxes from old wood.

Set plants more closely together than you would in a bed, to give a more concentrated display, and remember that all containers, and hanging baskets in particular, are susceptible to drying out. In hot weather they may need watering more than once a day. A balanced liquid feed should be used for container-grown plants. Some special container composts have slow-release feeding in them. Don't use over-rich compost.

STILL MORE COLOUR FROM HARDY ANNUALS

An inexpensive feature to provide colour is a hardy annual border. Hardy annuals are sown directly into the ground where they are to flower in April and May.

Preparation of beds should be thorough and the soil texture reasonably fine. Sticky clay soil should have sand added. Light sandy soils benefit from well-rotted organic matter. Rake level and provide a firm surface by treading, with general fertilizer added lightly. Early

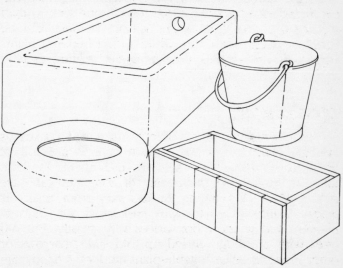

FIG 4 Suitable plant containers come in all shapes and sizes, and many successful containers can be made by converting discarded objects such as old sinks, buckets and even tyres. An attractive window box can be made from surplus wood.

preparation of borders allowing weeds to develop, then using a contact weed-killer, is a good technique *before* sowing. White sand can mark out a patchwork 'quilt' design for different varieties, allowing around 1 sq m (4 sq ft) per patch.

Seed can be broadcast in the patches or sown in drills. Sown broadcast, seed can be lightly covered by using a fine riddle, and the ground firmed with the back of a spade. Drills should be 20 cm (8 in) apart, seed sown thinly, drills closed and the soil packed down.

Planning the border means putting taller types at the back, shorter ones at the front. Ideally, write labels which indicate where each is to be sown. Thin out to 15–20 cm (6–8 in) apart when seedlings have germinated. As seedlings develop, support with twigs as necessary. The main problem is bad germination, due to varying weather and poor soil preparation.

BULBS IN YOUR GARDEN

Bulbs such as tulips and hyacinths are relatively expensive for spring bedding. Tulips can be lifted and saved for re-planting but it is better to buy bulbs for naturalization in shrub borders, lawns and odd corners. Once planted they will give pleasure for years to come. Look out for snowdrops, crocuses, scilla and bluebells, muscari (grape hyacinth), chionodoxa (glory of the snow) and of course narcissi or daffodils.

For summer bedding try liliums (which benefit from lifting, division and re-planting occasionally), montbretias and gladioli. Winter aconites and cyclamen are useful in the rock garden.

Bulbs are mainly sold in the autumn but if you are prepared to wait until the end of the season you may pick up a bargain. Do check that the bulbs are still firm and have not deteriorated in store.

HERBACEOUS PERENNIALS

Perennials give colour for many years and are an excellent investment. Most are relatively hardy, but can fall prey to slugs and rots in damp areas. Vermin can be troublesome. Many plants are raised from seeds, and from dividing existing plants. An excellent idea to buy a collection at bargain prices.

While it is usual to have a border, some gardeners prefer to put perennials between shrubs. This not only provides colour but the shrubs give shelter and support.

PLANNING AND SOIL PREPARATION

Sunny but sheltered beds are desirable, and the soil should be weed-free. Herbaceous perennials will be in one place for a long time, so dig in compost, well-rotted manure or clean organic matter to give the ground some body.

It is wise to check whether the border needs lime, and it should be cultivated to a good depth. Prior to planting, scatter on a slow-acting fertilizer such as fish and bone meal.

Set out plants in autumn or early spring. Groups of three plants 30–45 cm (12–18 in) apart is usual. Planting should be firm, followed by watering. Support will be needed, apart from low-growing types, by twigs or canes, with green twine run between them; it is hopeless to let herbaceous plants flop before they are staked. Some gardeners mulch with organic materials and fork this in lightly in early spring.

RAISING PLANTS YOURSELF

Herbaceous perennials can be propagated successfully in a number of ways, the method depending on the plant type. A good selection of herbaceous plants is available from seed (see below), possibly sown in a vacant cold frame, in May or June, but germination can be erratic. Michaelmas daisies and delphiniums grow well from stem cuttings, rooted in sandy soil in the spring. Many herbaceous plants can be split into smaller clumps, an operation best done in spring. Not only is this an economic way of acquiring new plants, it is beneficial to the plants themselves. Root cuttings can be taken from anemones, oriental poppies, eryngiums, echinops and phlox. Such cuttings are usually taken in early autumn, sections of root 2–5 cm (1–2 in) in length being laid flat in boxes of sandy soil. Layering is suitable for woody perennials, by which branches are secured into the ground with a hair grip or similar restrainer until roots have developed.

EASILY GROWN HERBACEOUS PERENNIALS WHERE SEED IS READILY AVAILABLE

Type	Height	Colour	Flowering
Acanthus mollis	90 cm (3 ft)	white/ purple	July/August
Achillea mille-folium	75 cm (2½ ft)	red	July/August
Alstroemeria Ligtu hybrids	75–90 cm (2½–3 ft)	various	summer
Alyssum	10–20 cm (4–8 in)	yellow	early summer
Anemone 'Mona Lisa' (sow in spring) excellent new cut-flower plant	45 cm (1½ ft)	various	autumn
Aquilegia	50 cm (20 in)	various	early summer
Arabis	10 cm (4 in)	rose, white, carmine	early summer
Aubrieta	10 cm (4 in)	blue, mauves	spring

Type	Height	Colour	Flowering
Auricula	15 cm (6 in)	mixed	spring
Campanula carpatica	20–30 cm (8–12 in)	blue/white	summer
Carnations Floriston	60 cm (2 ft)	various	summer
Catmint (*Nepeta*)	40 cm (16 in)	blue	summer
Christmas rose (*Helleborus niger*)	30 cm (1 ft)	white	winter
Coreopsis	45–75 cm (1½–2½ ft)	yellow	late summer
Day lily (*Hemerocallis*)	30–60 cm (1–2 ft)	various	summer
Delphinium	75–150 cm (2½–5 ft)	various	most of summer
Dianthus	30 cm (1 ft)	various	most of summer
Doronicum	60 cm (2 ft)	yellow	early summer
Double daisy (*Bellis perennis*)	15 cm (6 in)	various	summer
Erigeron	60 cm (2 ft)	blue/pink	most of summer
Foxglove	1.2 m (4 ft)	various	summer
Gaillardia	75 cm (2½ ft)	yellow/red	most of summer
Geum	60 cm (2 ft)	yellow, crimson	early summer
Globe thistle	1.2 m (4 ft)	blue/pink	most of summer
Gypsophila paniculata	60 cm (2 ft)	white	most of summer
Helenium	1 m (3½ ft)	yellow	mid summer
Heliopsis	120 cm (4 ft)	yellow	mid summer
Heuchera	40 cm (16 in)	various	early summer
Himalayan poppy (*Meconopsis baileyii*)	60–90 cm (2–3 ft)	blue	late summer

Type	Height	Colour	Flowering
Hollyhock	1.8–2.4 m (6–8 ft)	various	mid summer
Iris versicolor	60 cm (2 ft)	blue	early summer
Liatrus	60 cm (2 ft)	rose/ purple	summer
Linum	60 cm (2 ft)	blue	mid summer
Lupin	60–90 cm (2–3 ft)	various	early summer
Lychnis chalcedonica	90 cm (3 ft)	scarlet	mid summer
Monarda	75 cm (2½ ft)	various	mid summer
Phlox	60 cm (2 ft)	various	mid summer
Poppy	45 cm (1½ ft)	various	mid summer
Potentilla	30 cm (1 ft)	red	early summer
Sea holly	60 cm (2 ft)	silver blue	most of summer
Sidalcea	1 m (3½ ft)	various	mid summer
Statice	60 cm (2 ft)	blue	mid summer
Sweet pea, perennial	sprawling	various	all summer
Veronica teucrium	30 cm (1 ft)	blue	early summer

CHRYSANTHEMUMS

Chrysanthemums used to be avoided by gardeners with limited time. Now they are swinging back into popularity, especially the hardy border types. Planted in well-prepared land around 30 cm (12 in) apart in April/May they provide a superb amount of cut blooms. Later flowering types can be grown in pots and lifted into a greenhouse in September/October. They can be retained for many years, rooting cuttings in the spring from over-wintered stools. An excellent long-term investment.

COST-SAVING SUMMARY

The key to economy and yet achieving colour in the garden is growing plants from seed. If this is impractical the mail order catalogues may be used to make good savings on many items.

CHAPTER 8

GETTING VALUE OUT OF GREENHOUSES, FRAMES OR CLOCHES

To get full value from greenhouses, frames or cloches it is necessary to make the most use of them without incurring high heating costs.

COST OF GREENHOUSE GARDENING

A greenhouse, polythene structure or conservatory is a protective device to provide a more congenial climate for plants. Glass, polythene, PVC, fibreglass or polycarbonate all transmit heat from the sun. Reflected back by plants, ground or benches, this heats the atmosphere. As the sun is not shining all the time, artificial heat is needed to balance the temperature. The alternative is a completely unheated greenhouse, which considerably limits the scope of production. Because transparent materials transmit sun heat so effectively, there can be periods when too much is transmitted, and ventilation will be required to avoid overheating in summer.

The following are issues to take into account:
1. Size of greenhouse. The bigger the greenhouse, the more costly to heat.

2. Quality of construction; a leaky greenhouse with a cheap type of glazing system will become expensive to run.
3. The region, with regard to sunshine, average temperatures, weather pattern and exposure.
4. What the greenhouse or structure is composed of, whether glass, polythene, PVC, fibreglass or double-skinned polycarbonate.
5. The type of heating and the fuel involved, whether coal, oil or gas, electricity, or other fuel such as wood or straw systems which are seldom very practical on a small scale.
6. The required temperature level at different seasons, which is dependent on the uses to which the greenhouse will be put.

HEATING REQUIREMENTS

Measurement of surface area is the only accurate way of calculating heat requirements. Each specific material has its own thermal properties. Heat demand is still commonly calculated in British Thermal Units (BTUs).

AVERAGE SIZE OF HEATER FOR MODERATELY HEATED SPAN ROOF GLASS-TO-GROUND GREENHOUSE

1.8 × 1.2 m (6 × 4 ft)	1.25 kW	4 × 2.4 m	(14 × 8 ft)	3.25 kW
1.8 × 1.8 m (6 × 6 ft)	1.4 kW	4.8 × 3 m	(16 × 10 ft)	3.8 kW
2.4 × 1.8 m (8 × 6 ft)	1.5 kW	5.5 × 3.5 m	(18 × 12 ft)	4.6 kW
3 × 1.8 m (10 × 6 ft)	2.0 kW	6 × 3.5 m	(20 × 12 ft)	5.5 kW
3.5 × 2.4 m (12 × 8 ft)	2.75 kW			

1 kW = 1 unit of electricity = 3412 BTUs

Heaters have outputs stated in BTUs or kWs. The object is to calculate the heat requirement and relate this to the size of heater, for the temperature range selected. What the average gardener wants if the respective costs of providing heat by different fuels. A convenient measure for the output of heat is the therm, being 100,000 BTUs, or just over 20 kW.

METHODS OF HEATING

Solid fuel Using solid fuel at an average of £6 for 50 kg (approximately 1 cwt) and taking boiler efficiency at 50–60 per cent, the cost per therm works out about 75–80p. With simple boilers, a lot of heat goes up the flue and one has the labour of firing the boiler and cleaning out ashes. In many districts, however, cheaper fuels are available and there are gardeners prepared to undertake the work. Bear in mind that burning coal can mean smoke, which can create problems in certain areas.

Oil and paraffin The main fuel for small green-houses or structures is paraffin. Bought in small quantities, this can be as much as £1.85 a gallon and works out, taking the average efficiency of paraffin-burning stoves, at around £1.50 a therm.

The figures change dramatically if you have light oil for heating the home supplied in bulk, when you are possibly buying oil for around 50p a gallon; heating works out at about 40p a therm. Only larger heating units can burn light oil. Bear in mind that there is a difference in grades, and for flueless stoves paraffin is invariably recommended.

Gas Gas is bought by the therm. If you pay 30–40p a therm, and burn this at high efficiency, it will cost about 50–60p a therm. Bottled gas will cost more, possibly

25–30 per cent. There is much to be said for gas: it lends itself to automatic burning, but there is the risk of sulphur damage.

Electricity This is ideal, lending itself to automatic control through a thermostat. It depends what you pay, standard charges being around 6–7p a unit, with off-peak around half of that. But if the temperature is not to drop appreciably when off-peak heat is not available, provision has to be made for a switch over to standard rate. With 29 kW in a therm this could bring out the cost of greenhouse heating at £1.75 a therm at standard rate.

CALCULATING RUNNING COSTS OF HEATING SYSTEMS

These figures relate to hourly demands. In simple terms, if the heat demand is 1 kW an hour, a heater operating for 24 hours would use 24 kW. The setting of the heat level and the particular location are vital issues.

Taking average figures across the country, not more than a 10 per cent demand is usually needed for the 6°C degree (45°F) minimum temperature level. With electricity, costs of 14–20p a day for a small greenhouse with a 1.25 kW demand are average with paraffin slightly cheaper.

Whatever greenhouse you have, lining with bubble polythene can save money if you are heating it, or provide a warmer overall atmosphere if you are not. Remember *not* to cover up ventilators totally, especially if you are using paraffin heaters. Bubble polythene costs £1.30–1.50 per linear metre, 1.5 m (5 ft) wide. Fixing clips for aluminium greenhouses are about £1.75 for 50.

YEAR-ROUND USE OF THE GREENHOUSE

Programmes for greenhouses vary enormously, but the following is typical:

February/March–April raising bedding or vegetable plants, growing early vegetables such as lettuce. With a propagator this can be highly cost effective.

April/May–September growing tomatoes, cucumbers, peppers. Minimum heat required.

October/November late flowering chrysanthemums, for cut blooms. Minimum heat required.

December–February winter lettuce *in good light areas*, plus over-wintering of half-hardy plants. Frost protection only required.

Other salad crops include tomatoes, cucumbers, peppers, and beans as tall crops; lettuce, radish, mustard, cress, and spring onions as low-growing crops.

Vines and other fruits cost nothing in the way of heating but are cost effective only in the larger greenhouse or conservatory with room to spare.

With benching and basic heating, a range of pot plants can be grown. With bedding and pot plants, quantity is the key issue. Much can be done in the home by raising seedlings at light, warm windows with no extra heat.

PROPAGATORS AND UNHEATED FRAMES

Electric propagators are remarkably cheap to run and, where space or budget does not extend to a greenhouse or conservatory, can be helpful for germinating seed a little earlier. They can also be used to supply a few degrees of extra heat to more tender seedlings within a greenhouse.

Cold frames and cloches, inexpensive and easy to construct, suit vegetables, or hardier flowers such as rock plants and perennials. They are ideal for early crops of lettuce, carrots, onions, French beans, and low-growing strawberries. Typical prices of cold frames and cloches are discussed in Chapter 3.

CROPS UNDER GLASS

Exactly what you choose to grow will depend on room available and personal preference. It is not always easy to argue for home-grown produce on a purely economic basis, especially when growing on a small scale, but freshness, flavour and sense of satisfaction should also be taken into account.

The following are a few of the more popular choices for growing under glass.

TOMATOES

In the enthusiasm to grow these, the cost of actual production compared to buying is sometimes overlooked. Costs can mount to between £1.50 and £2.50 per plant, producing 2–5 kg (5–10 lb) of tomatoes.

Anywhere with good light, reasonable warmth, and enough room will do for tomatoes. A greenhouse or polythene structure suits tall tomatoes, but warm districts can get reasonable results outside. Dwarf or patio-type tomatoes can be grown in pots or hanging baskets, and are ideal for frames and cloches.

It is unwise to crowd tomatoes into a small area. About 60 × 60 cm (2 × 2 ft) per plant is ideal, so a greenhouse measuring 2.4 × 1.8 m (8 ft × 6 ft), will accommodate 12 plants. A growbag will accommodate three plants.

Tomatoes are easy to raise from seed, but it takes between six and 12 weeks. For earliest crops, sow in a propagator in February; otherwise wait until late February or early March. A really early crop is unlikely to be cost effective, if a lot is spent on heating, and the price of compost for successive potting on will have to be taken into consideration.

Buying in plants saves a lot of fuss and bother, but at 30–50p per plant will usually be more expensive, and there will be less choice than from a seed catalogue. Currently, 'Blizzard' or 'Abunda' are popular, and older types like 'Ailsa Craig', 'Moneymaker', and 'Alicante' are still favoured. Small-fruited varieties such as 'Sweet 100' are becoming popular, as are 'Totem' or 'Tumbler' for pots or hanging baskets.

To encourage a good crop, plants will have to be staked and pinched out (unless a dwarf variety), given copious water and regular high-potash feeds. Stripping off foliage round a truss will aid ripening, and late tomatoes can be brought indoors to ripen. Persistently green fruit can be made into chutney, so waste is minimal.

CUCUMBERS

Cucumbers make a useful follow-on crop on greenhouse benches, after bedding plants. They can also be grown in growbags (two or three per bag) or in heaps of soil and manure. Yield per plant depends on time of planting. If planted in April and given night heat each plant may produce 12–15 fruits but later plantings only 6–8 fruits per plant. A more cost-effective method is to take out planting holes in vacant cold frames. Fill with well-rotted manure, set out plants in May or early June, training growth to the corners of the frame. A mulch of straw or black polythene will keep the fruit off the ground and avoid waste. In warm areas, cucumbers may be grown out of doors, with a little cloche protection at first.

Pick all-female varieties for the greenhouse work; for frames or outdoors, select ridge varieties which have a hardier constitution. Useful varieties are 'Venlo', 'Long Green Ridge' and 'Perfection'.

Like tomatoes, cucumber plants will need a regular supply of water and feed, although a more highly nitrogenous one than tomatoes.

LETTUCE

With a little planning, your garden can keep you supplied with lettuce for most of the year. Use a section of the greenhouse in the border from February to May, following on in frames or cloches from April to May, with outdoor production in summer. Seed sown in August produces plants for the greenhouse in September, to mature in December with frost protection and little more. Protection fleece helps early outdoor crops.

The trick with lettuce is not to sow too much at once, which will result in a glut, and to choose the right variety for the time of year. Many of the 'speciality' lettuces which are so expensive in the shops can easily be raised from seed at a fraction of the cost. It pays to consult seed catalogues as new varieties appear constantly.

OTHER CROPS

A wide range of vegetables can be grown in greenhouses, including spring onions, radishes and early turnips, sown during February or March. Parsley does well in pots which can be lifted in during the autumn. If there is room, climbing French beans sown in March will give an early crop. Peppers and aubergines can also be successfully raised in a greenhouse, and are especially satisfying, because shop prices are usually so high.

Forcing rhubarb provides an early bite. Lift a few crowns in November or December and pack them in with some peat under the greenhouse bench, with light excluded by black polythene. This produces succulent blanched shoots, at a time when they are pricey in shops.

COST-SAVING SUMMARY

Avoid high heating costs and use your home or smaller, heated propagators where possible. Plan your greenhouse or frame cropping programme in advance.

CHAPTER 9

VEGETABLES AND FRUITS OUT OF DOORS

Whether it is worth growing vegetables and fruit in your garden is something to be considered objectively. Ideally, you need good, well-prepared land open to the sun with no serious weed or drainage problems.

It is remarkable what can be done with a bit of forethought. Frequently, fruit can be grown up against a wall, where they do not take up much room and can be very rewarding. Salads or mini-vegetables can also often be grown without taking up a great deal of room.

To grow any quantity of fruit and vegetables and save on the shopping bill means setting out with purpose, and this is most definitely worth while if you have space or perhaps an allotment. It is possible with good planning to have a fair degree of self-sufficiency over the full year. Let's look at vegetables first.

HOME-GROWN VEGETABLES

CROP ROTATION

One of the first rules for vegetables is to move them around on a regular basis, or you can end up with persistent diseases such as club root or pests such as potato cyst eelworm. A typical method of rotation is as shown in Fig. 5.

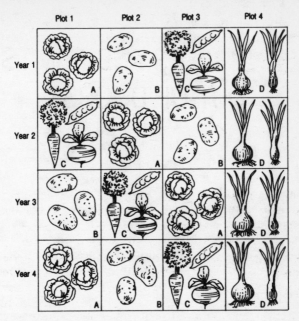

FIG 5 A typical crop rotation system for vegetables.

WEEDS

While they don't totally inhibit growing, weeds make things difficult. Annual weeds can be tacked with regular hoeing and hand pulling, but deep-rooted perennial weeds are not so easy to get rid of. It is easy to rush into growing vegetables without proper ground preparation. There is much to be said for a period of bare fallowing, when ground is left fallow and hoed regularly over a period, ideally in the spring or early summer.

If you are keen on organic growing and want to keep expenses down, why not sow out green crops such as Italian or Hungarian rye grass, vetch, mustard and cress, and dig these into the ground as a green manure, ideally before they seed. This controls weeds to a certain extent and improves the soil texture. One way of overcoming weeds is to grow vegetables through black plastic or special paper mulches.

FEEDING THE CROPS

You are not going to get good results unless you feed the ground. It is common sense to keep ground in good condition by adding a mixture of compost and organic manures, which can be bought or may be obtained locally at little cost. Provided you are not an out-and-out organic person, it is surely logical to use limited amounts of fertilizers in addition to organic materials, if used sparingly and locally to the crops being grown. Otherwise, you can waste money (see Chapter 4).

Many vegetables like a fairly sweet soil, which may mean adjusting the pH by adding lime. Remember that potatoes don't like too much lime.

PROBLEMS

If you are growing a range of vegetables, you must look out for various problems. These include club root of the cabbage family, which distorts the roots and reduces crops of brassicas to almost nil. Cyst eelworm on potatoes is a very persistent pest which can last for years and years. Slugs are always around and may need evasive action. In addition, you will almost certainly have trouble with cabbage root fly, and carrot fly, if you don't take preventive measures, plus caterpillars eating the leaves of brassicas later in the season. (See Appendix A for control measures.)

YOUR VEGETABLE TIMETABLE

While not critical, good timing is common sense. It is pointless to sow too early and risk frost damage, or too late and not give crops enough time to mature. Reference Table 1 shows optimum time for sowing, preferred soil type and conditions, and expected harvest.

TABLE 1: GROWING VEGETABLES

Crop	Ease of growing	Timing	Soil	Region	Period of harvesting	Approx yield per plant
Asparagus	Preparing beds and raising plants can be time-consuming; weed control can be constant	Sow seed in spring, plant the following spring in rows 1.5 m (5 ft) apart	Medium, light peaty	Best in warm areas	Mid/late spring	0.7 kg (1.5 lb)
Beans						
– broad	A cheap, easy crop to grow	Sow in March/early April in rows 1 m (3 ft) apart	All soils	Very hardy	Mid-summer to autumn; freezes well	100–250 g (4–8 oz)
– dwarf	As for broad beans	Sow in early/mid-May in rows 1 m (3 ft) apart	All soils	Best in warm areas	Summer to autumn; freezes well	1 kg (2 lb)
– runner	Support means work and some cost	Sow early/mid-May or in pots early or under protection, sow in rows 2 m (7 ft) apart or at the base of beanpoles	All soils	Best in warm areas	Late summer to autumn; freezes	200 g (6 oz)
Beetroot	Cheap and easy	Sow in May in drills 30 cm (12 in) apart, thin out as required	Most soils	Crops well	Stores well	up to 225 g (8 oz)
Broccoli	(see Cauliflower)					

Crop	Ease of growing	Timing	Soil	Region	Period of harvesting	Approx yield per plant
Brussels sprouts	One of the most rewarding crops to grow at low cost	Sow in seedbed in greenhouse or in cold frame in March/April for planting May/June around 45 cm (18 in) apart	All soils	Everywhere but extreme exposure	Autumn to spring; freezes well	560 g (1¼ lb)
Cabbage	Apart from fighting cabbage fly and caterpillars, a low-cost crop	For spring cabbage sow in August, plant out 30 cm (12 in) apart	All soils	Most areas	Good choice of varieties and types; gives continuous supplies	up to 680 g (1½ lb)
Carrot	Carrot fly a constant problem; weeding is demanding	Sow in April in drills 30 cm (12 in) apart; thin as required	Best in light soils	All areas, early crops under glass	Stores well and helps the household budget	very variable according to type
Cauliflower/ Broccoli/ Calabrese	Low cost crop to grow	As for Brussels sprouts	Soils with a bit of body in them	Winter broccoli best in mild areas	Grow different varieties for continuity	2 kg (4 lb)
Celery, self-blanching and ordinary	Self-blanching easiest and cheapest to grow	Sow in greenhouse in April for planting out 30 cm (12 in) in May; others in deep trenches for earthing up, 30 cm (12 in) between plants	Best in light or peaty land	All regions, revels in cloche protection	From mid-summer on; freezes	250 g (8 oz)

Cucumber	Easy but needs a lot of watering	Sow in greenhouse in April for planting May/June around 1.5 m (5 ft) apart in cold frame	Likes good local preparation	Best in frames or greenhouses	Mid-summer and autumn	2 kg (4 lb)
Endive	Easy crop	Sow July/August for winter crop, allow 30 cm (12 in) when planting out or thinning down	All soils	Most areas	Autumn to winter, depending on climate	See lettuce
Gourds or Squashes	Easy	Essential to wait until all frost is past, sow seed in greenhouse, plant out allowing plenty of room	Well-drained soil	Warm corners best	Late summer to autumn	2 kg (4 lb) or more
Herbs	Simple; ideal for cheap tasty tit-bits	Wide range available, grown similarly to herbaceous plants or in small beds, most can be sown in greenhouse or cold frame in spring	All soils	All regions	Long period, always useful	
Kale	One of the lowest-cost crops to grow, giving a good return	See cabbage	All soils	All regions	All winter, to mid-spring	0.5 kg (1 lb)

80	Crop	Ease of growing	Timing	Soil	Region	Period of harvesting	Approx yield per plant
	Leeks	Easy to grow; very valuable in winter for the soup pot	Sow in greenhouse in March for planting out 30 cm (12 in) in May/June	Rich soil for best results	All regions	Very long period	up to 250 g (8 oz)
	Lettuce	Simple and can save a lot of money for the salad bowl	Sow in succession from March onwards, sow in drills 30 cm (12 in) apart, thin as required	All soils, but must be fertile	Early and late crops need protection	Successional cropping over long period to get full value	up to 350 g (12 oz)
	Marrow/ Courgette	Demanding for watering	As for gourds	Good soils	All regions: likes protection	Mid-summer to autumn	variable
	Mustard/and Cress	Easy to grow	Usually sown broadcast in small batches from April onwards out of doors or in boxes or in greenhouse borders during winter months	Best in pots or boxes	All areas	Long period if sown regularly	

Onions	Easy; saves a lot of money for the salad bowl	Sow seeds in March for setting out in April/May around 30 cm (12 in) apart, plant sets 5 cm (2 in) apart in rows 30 cm (12 in) apart	Rich soils only	All areas	Spring onions late spring, bulb onions from late summer; store well	50–100 g (2–4 oz)
Parsnip	Easy and cheap to grow	One of the first seeds to sow in March or April, in rows at least 30 cm (12 in) apart, thin as required	All soils	All areas	From early autumn, over long periods	Very variable but can be up to 1 kg (2 lb)
Peas	Easy; superb and valuable crop	Sow from late March on, in succession in shallow drills at least 1 m (3 ft) apart giving more space for taller varieties	All soils	All regions: early under cloches	From summer to autumn; freeze well	250 g (8 oz)

Crop	Ease of growing	Timing	Soil	Region	Period of harvesting	Approx yield per plant
Potatoes	Worth growing only in reasonable quantities	Grow in shallow drills to be earthed up; set tubers 1 m (3 ft) apart, sprout early types before planting, normal time of setting out is during April	All soils	All areas	From early/mid-summer onwards; store well	2.5–3.5 kg (6–8 lb)
Radish	Easy: excellent for salads	Sow in succession from March onward in drills 30 cm (12 in) apart, thin as required and use thinnings	All soils	All regions: early under protection	Late spring onwards	30–40 g (1–1½ oz)
Shallots	Simple and cheap to grow	As for onion sets	All soils	All regions	From late summer; store well	5–6 bulbs

Crop	Ease of growing	Timing	Soil	Region	Period of harvesting	Approx yield per plant
Spinach	Easy and good for feeding a lot of mouths	Sow in succession from early April in drills at least 30 cm (12 in) apart	All soils	All areas	Long period, according to type and variety	250 g (8 oz)
Sweet corn	Fairly easy and saves on the household budget	Start in greenhouse or frame, in pots and plant out in late April/early May around 45 cm (18 in) apart	All soils	Likes warmth to mature	From early/late summer; freezes well	3–5 cobs
Tomatoes	Demanding	See page 71	Rich soil	Warm areas for outdoor crops; best results in greenhouse	Early summer to mid autumn	1–1.25 kg (2–3 lb) (outdoors)
Turnips/ Swedes	Easy but club root troublesome; excellent money-saving vegetable	Sow early turnips from April on in drills 30 cm (12 in) apart, swedes in May in drills 45 cm (18 in) apart, use thinnings of early turnips and thin swedes as required	All soils	All areas	Autumn to spring	0.5–1 kg (1½–2½ lb)

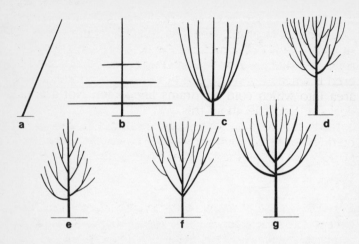

FIG 6 *Fruit can be trained into a number of shapes, many of which will reduce the amount of growing space required. (a) cordon; (b) espalier; (c) fan; (d) bush; (e) pyramid; (f) half standard; (g) standard. Check that the fruit tree has been grafted on to a suitable rootstock.*

GROWING FRUIT IN THE GARDEN

Some fruits take up a lot of room whereas others can be fitted into odd corners very effectively and be remarkably productive, too. Many, such as apples and pears, can be stored for long periods, others deep freeze beautifully, and of course one can make jams or preserves. In other words, you certainly get full value out of fruit (Fig. 6).

EXPOSURE

One of the biggest problems for fruit is exposure, especially when trying to grow apples, pears and plums. In addition, there is the pollination period to consider when, if the blooms are dashed, you are not going to get fruit. The best compromise is to grow dwarf-growing fruit such as blueberries or strawberries and to a lesser extent currants or gooseberries. Even in a very exposed situation, fruit can sometimes be grown advantageously against a sheltered wall. Something else to be considered is whether your garden lies in a frost pocket, a low area into which cold air drains like water. Not a great deal can be done about this.

Birds can be a serious problem, and a fruit-cage or netting may be the only answer in certain circumstances. Fruit grown against the wall can often be effectively netted.

SOILS

Bearing in mind the long-term nature of fruit, with the exception of strawberries, it is worth taking the time to improve soil fertility by digging in clean organic matter. Drainage, too, is something to take into account. Once planted there is much to be said for mulching the fruit area, and wood or forest bark, although expensive, is worth while in the long term. Generally speaking any good organic matter which comes to hand should be considered.

Black polythene mulching is very popular for strawberries, as is growing them in barrels or towers. It is remarkable what yield can be achieved in a very small area.

BUYING STOCK

All garden supply centres stock a wide range of fruit trees and bushes these days, and most of the stock is certified and of high quality. Many soft fruits lend themselves to self-propagation, particularly stawberries with runners, and raspberries with suckers. Currants and gooseberries are simple to propagate by taking autumn cuttings. With currants it is important *not* to propagate stock which has big bud mite trouble (indicated by swollen buds).

TIMES OF PLANTING

Container-grown trees and bushes can be planted any time. Bare root specimens of currants, gooseberries and strawberries are better planted in autumn or early spring. Local soil preparation may be required, and bear in mind that the life of a strawberry bed is going to be three or four years, and trees and bushes very much longer.

Crop rotation should be practised to avoid carrying over troubles such as root rots.

The following table outlines the main fruit and their vital statistics.

COST-SAVING SUMMARY

Potential savings will be limited by space available.

Growing only a few varieties well that will be well used in the kitchen is better than trying to grow a bit of everything.

TABLE 2: GROWING FRUIT

Fruit	Form	Distance between rows	Distance between plants	Aspect on walls	Comments
Apple	cordon/'Ballerina'*	1.5–1.8 m (5–6 ft)	90 cm (3 ft)	any	medium soil well-drained (1)
	espalier	—	3.5–4.5 m (12–15 ft)	any	
	dwarf and spire				
	pyramid	2.5 m (8 ft)	1.2–1.5 m (4–5 ft)	any	Dessert varieties best in warm areas
	bush	3.5–4.5 m (12–15 ft)	3.5–4.5 m (12–15 ft)	any	
	half standard	6 m (20 ft)	6 m (20 ft)	any	
	standard	7.5 m (25 ft)	7.5 m (25 ft)	any	
Apricot	fan	—	4.5 m (15 ft)	S or W	Open soil, well-limed, needs warmth (1)
Blackberry	fan	1.8 m (6 ft)	3–4.5 m (10–15 ft)	any	Any soil, grow in most areas (2)
Blueberry*	bush	1 m (3–4 ft)	1 m (3–4 ft)	any	Acid peat, most areas (2,4,6)
Cherry, sweet	fan	—	4.5–6 m (15–20 ft)	W, S or E	Bird protection essential good soil (1)
	bush*	5.5 m (18 ft)	5.5 m (18 ft)	W, S or E	
	half standard	7.5–9 m (25–30 ft)	7.5 m (25 ft)	W, S or E	
	standard	9–12 m (30–40 ft)	9–12 m (30–40 ft)	W, S or E	
sour	fan	—	4.5–5.5 m (15–18 ft)	any	Well-limed soil
	bush	3.5 m (12 ft)	3.5 m (12 ft)	any	
	half standard	5.5 m (18 ft)	5.5 m (18 ft)	any	
Cobnut	bush	3.5 m (12 ft)	3.5 m (12 ft)	any	Bird protection needed Not too rich or grows wild (2, 4, 6)
Currant, black	bush	1.5 m (5 ft)	1.8 m (6 ft)	any	Does well on rich ground, all areas, makes good jam (2)
	cordon	—	60 cm (2 ft)	any	
red	bush*	1.5 m (5 ft)	1.5 m (5 ft)	any	Light open soil
or white	cordon	—	60 cm (2 ft)	any	

Fruit	Form	Distance between rows	Distance between plants	Aspect on walls	Comments
Damson	bush	3.5–4.5 m (12–15 ft)	3.5–4.5 m (12–15 ft)	any	Heavy soil best (1)
	half standard	3.5–6 m (12–20 ft)	5.5–6 m (18–20 ft)	any	
Fig	fan	—	4.5–6 m (15–20 ft)	S or W	Medium porous soil, needs warmth to ripen, best in greenhouse (2)
Gooseberry*	cordon	—	60 cm (2 ft)	any	Medium-light soil, plenty of potash, good for jam or tarts (2)
	espalier	1.5 m (5 ft)	1.8 m (6 ft)	any	
	bush	1.8 m (6 ft)	1.5 m (5 ft)	any	
Grape	cordon	1.8 m (6 ft)	1.2 m (4 ft)	S or W	Not too rich soil, best in greenhouse (2)
	espalier	2.5 m (8 ft)	3.5–4.5 m (12–15 ft)	S or W	
Loganberry*	fan	1.8 m (6 ft)	2.5 m (8 ft)	any	Medium soil (4, 6)
Medlar	bush	3.5 m (12 ft)	3.5 m (12 ft)	any	Any reasonable soil (1)
Peach/nectarine	fan	—	4.5–5.5 m (15–18 ft)	SE to SW	Light loam, warm areas only (1)
Pear	cordon	1.8 m (6 ft)	90 cm (3 ft)	S, W or E	Heavy loam best (1)
	espalier	—	5.5 m (18 ft)	S, W or E	
	pyramid	3–3.5 m (10–12 ft)	3.5 (12 ft)	S, W or E	
	bush*	3.5 m (12 ft)	3.5 m (12 ft)	S, W or E	
	standard	6–9 m (20–30 ft)	6–9 m (20–30 ft)	S, W or E	
Plums	fan	—	4.5–6 m (15–20 ft)	any	Heavy loam, (1) grows well in most areas, superb for jam
	bush*	3–3.5 m (10–12 ft)	3–3.5 m (10–12 ft)	any	
	half standard	6–7 m (20–24 ft)	6–7 m (20–24 ft)	any	

Quince	bush	3–3.5 m (10–12 ft)	3–3.5 m (10–12 ft)	any	Any good soil (2, 3)
	half standard	5.5 m (18 ft)	5.5 m (18 ft)	any	
Raspberry*	canes	1.5–1.8 m (5–6 ft)	45 cm (18 in)	any	Well-drained rich soil, deep-freezes well (4)
Strawberry*	plants	60–90 cm (2–3 ft)	30–45 cm (12–18 in)	any	Any reasonable well-drained soil (5)
Tayberry*	bush	as for raspberries	as for raspberries	any	Fresh, or for jam a 'must', does well in towns (2)
Walnut	standard	9 m (30 ft)	9 m (30 ft)	any	Any reasonable soil (1, 3)

* Most rewarding for small gardens.

Note: yields of all fruits are very variable.

Propagation: (1) Bud on stocks (2) Cuttings (3) Seeds (4) Division (5) Runners (6) Layers. Many can be propagated from seeds with varying results.

PESTICIDES AND WEEDKILLERS

Only around 4 per cent of gardeners do not use any chemicals in the garden. The majority accept that chemicals have a useful role, used strictly according to directions and as required. There are also bio-friendly chemicals and methods, although trials show that they are sometimes not too effective.

LITERATURE

Buy a current copy of *Garden Chemicals*, published by British Agrichemicals Association Ltd, 4 Lincoln Court, Lincoln Road, Peterborough PE1 2RP. Tel: 0733 349226, at a post-paid cost of £1.50 (1991–1992 edition). This is a full list of approved gardening chemicals. There are also many societies and groups who will be able to give advice.

The control of weeds is a complex subject. Many gardeners prefer not to use chemical weedkillers, relying on a hoe or mulching materials such as black polythene. There are many who do not object to a covering of weeds, as it is a more natural way of growing crops. Where weed control is felt to be important, there are basically two types of weedkillers. Those which kill by contact and those where the plant absorbs the chemical through its roots and leaves. Some weedkillers are highly systemic, which means the chemical is passed through the whole plant.

COST OF PEST, DISEASE AND
WEED CONTROL

It is sound advice to buy sensibly sized bags of chemicals, and store them safely in a suitably dry place. Avoid storing any type of garden chemicals beside plants or foods, and keep hormone weedkillers away from greenhouses. They can cause tremendous damage.

Symptoms	Bio-friendly treatment	Chemical treatment	Comment
Ants – heaps of soil and burrows which disturb seedlings	Pyrethrums most helpful	Diazinon/ pyrethrums/ Borax	More a nuisance than a menace, can generally be ignored.
Cabbage root fly – white maggots attack roots causing wilting and death of cabbages, sprouts, cauli-flowers, broccoli, radishes, etc.	Collars of tar paper round neck of plants, use of fleece or fine mesh to avoid entry of fly.	Bromophos/ Gamma HCH	A persistent pest, almost impossible to avoid without preventive measures.
Carrot fly – maggots attack roots. First symptoms are reddish tinge to leaves. Parsnips also attacked.	Sow thinly to avoid extensive thinning, use fleece or mesh to avoid entry of fly. Creosote-soaked ropes on sticks mask	Gamma HCH/ Bromophos	Thin sowing is cheapest and safest control method.

Symptoms	Bio-friendly treatment	Chemical treatment	Comment
	smell of carrots. Planting herbs, leeks, onions, salsify adjacent helps, as does growing quick-maturing varieties.		
Cutworms – caterpillars of various types sever stems of plants.	Hoeing and hand picking helpful, also putting out old toilet rolls into which caterpillars collect. Having a hedgehog very useful.	As for carrot fly.	Trapping with toilet roll method is highly cost effective.
Biting pests – attack cabbages and other crops.	Wide range of methods such as hand picking, planting herbs adjacent, allowing predators to develop by avoidance of spraying. *Bacillus thuringiensis* for cabbage butterfly is useful. Fleece materials help in avoiding entry of butterflies and moths.	Wide range of chemicals is available, including pyrethrums.	Very difficult to avoid caterpillar damage unless regular spraying or alternative methods carried out.

Symptoms	Bio-friendly treatment	Chemical treatment	Comment
White fly – attacks wide range of plants, particularly in greenhouses, sucking sap, exuding honeydew on which fungus grows.	Hanging up fly cards, growing French or African marigolds in greenhouse can greatly help, as can use of parasitic wasp, *Ercarsia formosa*.	A range of chemicals is offered, some of which are systemic (taken up by plant). Smoke cones useful in green-house.	Very difficult to control. Thorough cleaning of greenhouse at end of season essential.
Leatherjackets – large grey grubs, eating stems and roots.	Hand picking and trapping with cut turnip useful.	Gamma HCH/Phoxin/ Carbaryl on lawns.	Worst on areas recently turfed.
Onion fly – maggots eat into bulbs.	Fleece or herbs planted near onions useful. Avoid thinning.	Gamma HCH	Planting herbs achieves control.
Slugs and snails – eat everything in sight.	Avoid rubbish. Jam jars containing some beer and laid on side very effective.	Metalde-hyde/ Methiocarb pellets used regularly.	Impossible to control, especially in wet areas. Using lot of organic matter encourages slugs.
Wireworms – yellow grubs attack roots of many plants.	Trapping with cut turnip helps. Plant with aromatic herbs.	Phoxin/ Gamma HCH	Very difficult to get total control.
Sucking pests – very wide range of pests including aphids, blackfly,	Seaweed derived plant foods claimed to help, particularly if ladybirds	Wide range of chemicals, some of which are systemic.	Decide whether damage acute enough to start spraying. Companion

Symptoms	Bio-friendly treatment	Chemical treatment	Comment
whitefly, red spider and others. Attack leaves and shoots of many plants. Cause leaf speckling, distortion, stunted growth.	and other predators encouraged. Pyrethrum or Derris sprays can be effective, as can soft soap used regularly.	Possibly most effective is Malathion.	planting reasonably effective.

Common diseases

Fungal diseases generally, including mildew, black-spot, rusts etc. Wide range of symptoms, according to type; require consultation of disease chart for accurate identification.	Organic gardeners recommend various materials such as marestail or elder leaf tea, soft soap, and other mild fungicides. It is important to avoid congestion and excessively damp unventilated conditions in greenhouses.	Wide range of chemicals can be used, some of which are systemic. It is important to identify troubles accurately and refer to lists for correct chemical.	It is impossible to avoid fungal troubles in the garden, especially blackspot on roses. If total control is required, regular spraying is a must.
Club root – cabbages and other brassica roots are distorted and growth stunted, rendering crops useless.	Good drainage and heavy liming of ground useful.	Thiophanate methyl a useful pre-ventative.	Sour, wet ground should be avoided and crops rotated regularly.

INDEX